Memories of VMI

Memories of VMI

♦

Volume II

*Collected, Compiled, and Edited
by
Ursula Maria Mandel*

iUniverse, Inc.
New York Lincoln Shanghai

Memories of VMI
Volume II

All Rights Reserved © 2003 by Ursula Maria Mandel

No part of this book may be reproduced or transmitted in any form or by any means, graphic, electronic, or mechanical, including photocopying, recording, taping, or by any information storage retrieval system, without the written permission of the publisher.

iUniverse, Inc.

For information address:
iUniverse, Inc.
2021 Pine Lake Road, Suite 100
Lincoln, NE 68512
www.iuniverse.com

ISBN: 0-595-29559-2

Printed in the United States of America

To George C. Marshall

Contents

Foreword. xi
1   If I Only Had a Brain, *Pickering, Lance, '88* 1
2   A Further Version of the Famous Bomb Story, *Johnson, Paul, '58* . . 2
3   A Salute to the Commandant, *Seletz, Jules (Bromo), '53* 3
4   Arrival, *Strickler, Edmund, '62* 4
5   Attending a Fancy Dress Ball, *Meola, Warren, '52* 5
6   Backfire, *Montero, Josh, '04* 8
7   BD Mayo, *Prof of Math, Meola, Warren, '52* 10
8   Clean What? *Carr, Houston H. (Tex), '59* 14
9   Corps Trip, *Pickering, Lance, '88* 15
10 Cow on the Roof! *Ford, George, '54* 17
11 Cunning and Desperate, *Hanke, Erwin, '71* 19
12 Do You See What I See? *Carr, Houston H. (Tex) '59* 22
13 Double Trouble, *Lane, RB, '75* 23
14 Drinking Privileges, *Schwab, David, '73* 24
15 Fireworks Run in the Family, *Ford, George, '54* 25
16 First Number One, *Pickering, Lance, '88* 28
17 Football, *Woolwine, Sam E., '58* 30
18 Greasy Bird, *Hanke, Erwin, '71* 31
19 High Explosives, *Lash, Tony, '58* 33

20	Horizontal Lab, *Carr, Houston H. (Tex), '59*	34
21	How the Institute Got Buzzed, *Colvin, Tom, '53*	35
22	Images, *Carr, Houston H. (Tex), '59*	37
23	Jail Party, *Meola, Warren, '52*	39
24	Jersey Rat Goes Executive, *Hanke, Erwin, '71*	42
25	Jersey Rat Meets the General Committee, *Hanke, Erwin, '71*	44
26	Jersey Rat Meets the System, *Hanke, Erwin, '71*	46
27	Jiggs and Big N, *Carr, Houston H. (Tex), '59*	49
28	Just Let Me Sleep, *Southworth, Nathaniel (Aric), '94*	51
29	Just Trust Me, *Bradley, Cary, '75*	53
30	Kangaroo Mascot, *Carr, Houston H. (Tex), '59*	55
31	Keydet Wiley Coyote, *Carr, Houston H. (Tex), '59*	56
32	Late Dating a Mink, *Koontz, Warren, '53*	57
33	Lexington Express, *Noell, Bill, '53*	58
34	Life with Moe, *Schwab, David, '73*	61
35	Light the Tree, *Toler, Alan, '83*	63
36	Matriculation Day, *Pickering, Lance, '88*	64
37	Mickey Mouse, *Carr, Houston H. (Tex), '59*	66
38	Muscle Power, *Pomponio, Art, '59*	67
39	New Cadet Shoes, *Schwab, David, '73*	69
40	Nine Years Later, *Strickler, Edmund, '62*	70
41	Officer in Charge, *Carr, Houston H. (Tex), '59*	71
42	Out of the Frying Pan, *Hanke, Erwin, '71*	72
43	Penny Annoyance, *Toler, Alan, '83*	75
44	Prophesy, *Mackenzie, Bruce, '59*	76

45	Rain? *Fall, Eddie, '59*	77
46	Rat Bites, *Pickering, Lance, '88*	78
47	Regarding Nicknames, *Meola, Warren, '52*	80
48	Rice vs. LSU, *Meola, Warren, '52*	83
49	Room Change, *Koontz, Warren, '53*	86
50	Snakes in Barracks, *Meola, Warren, '52*	87
51	Snippets, *Lawson, Ray, '81*	89
52	Spirit Ball, *Fall, Eddie, '59*	91
53	State Police to the Rescue, *Old, Bill, no class year provided*	93
54	Tanks for the Memories, *Carr, Houston (Tex), '59*	94
55	Thanksgiving Day, 1951, *Meola, Warren, '52*	95
56	The Bomb and the Mullion, *Meola, Warren, '52*	98
57	The Cadre Sergeant, *Schwab, David, '73*	101
58	The Definitive Cannonball Story, *Hammond, Leroy, '57*	102
59	The Hook and the Tree, *Meola, Warren, '52*	104
60	The Inscrutable Dr. Chang, *Hanke, Erwin, '71*	106
61	Under Arrest, *Meola, Warren, '52*	108
62	VMI Commander Trips, *Carr, Houston H. (Tex), '59*	110
63	VMI Prelude to Real Life, *Hanke, Erwin, '71*	112
64	Welcome to the RDC, *Schwab, David, '73*	115
65	What Mercedes? *Eads, Matthew, '93*	116
66	Wrestling at SMA, *Meola, Warren, '52*	117
67	Ring Figure, *Strickler, Edmund, '62*	120
Lexicon for the Uninitiate		121
About the Author		123

Foreword

A Story

Sometimes, life works in mysterious ways. This may not come as a surprise to some of you, but it always amazes me.

When I taught at George Mason University, I would, now and then, have students from VMI.

Never heard of it!

"Where," I would ask them, "is VMI?"

They'd smile, at once sheepish and proud,

"In Lexington."

"And why are you here?"

"Because we're flunking English."

"Oh!"

At about that time, I began dating a man who—you guessed it—graduated from VMI (Fred Hauser, '53), though I found this out only weeks later, in a casual conversation with a mutual friend.

In the summer of '87, Fred and I decided to drive down the Blue Ridge Parkway all the way to North Carolina. When we got close to Lexington, I said:

"Let's get off here for just a little. I really want to see where my students go to school."

He gave me a sideways glance: "I have no interest in going to Lexington! These were, probably, the worst four years of my life. I have no interest in ever seeing this place again!"

But I won, and we drove down the mountain into Lexington about noon. We turned a corner in this quaint town, and he said:

"Oh, here's the Field House."

We took a right, up a very sharp curve, into VMI, and he said, "Oh, look. This little house was once a hospital. And, oh, look here, that's Crozet Hall, and…oh, Jackson Arch—and if you look inside barracks—there, right there—that was my room when I was a 3rd. And way up there—my rat room…and…"

By nine that night, we were still on Post. It seems that, the moment we drove into the place, Fred fell in love with it all over, and, essentially, he's not left it since. That first day, we had to scramble to find a place to stay, at ten at night. We spent the rest of our vacation in Lexington—mostly on Post and in every building I had access to.

I spent hours in the VMI Museum, with Fred explaining the history of a valiant place and of distinguished alumni, some of whom fought in WWII. I spent even more hours in the George C. Marshall Museum. I spent a long time in front of a picture of children, and I saw myself, at about that time, with the same cautious hopefulness and the reluctant smile. Had it not been for the genius of the Marshall plan, these children, including me, would not have survived.

I don't know what made me announce, on that day, August 2, 2001, that I would collect your memories of life at VMI. But I will never forget that spontaneous feeling of absolute certainty of purpose that accompanied my words. I know now what I didn't know then—that there was, is, of course, a connection between the museums, the general, and the child.

Payback time, maybe, for having been saved from oblivion, as I hoped to do with your stories. If I have my way, they will never go out of print.

As for the project itself, it was a pleasure! I loved getting your e-mails and writing back to you. I've made so many wonderful friends. I love your stories! I haven't laughed that hard in a long time.

Working on your stories, I tried to do my best to preserve your style and your memories as you wrote them to me. I interfered only where the grammatically challenged became obscure. If I made mistakes, if you find errors, take them with a dose of good will, good humor, and, above all, tolerance.

One of the things I hoped this project would do is to draw you closer together. And that has already begun, because friends who had not heard from one another in years have found one another again through this project.

You have something most people can only dream of—you belong to a beautiful place, a beautiful history, a beautiful people. You were and are so lucky.

Here then is Volume II of a beloved book.

Your Editor,
Ursula Maria Mandel

1

If I Only Had A Brain

Lance Pickering, '88

(Author's note: I've changed the names in this story to protect the *innocent.*) As a rat, you often have an upperclassman tell you to "sound-off." When receiving this command, a rat is supposed to yell his last name, initials, and hometown. Well, when I was a rat, my company had some pretty cheeky corporals who liked to have fun with the command of "sound-off." Of course, this fun was at our expense or, more properly, at the expense of three of my BR's.

One of my BR's was in the Glee Club and had a beautiful singing voice. Also, like all rats, he was pretty clueless, at least as far as the Thirds were concerned. So, he was given a special and unique way to answer the command of "sound-off." We would be in ranks or marching and some corporal would decide it was time for some "fun" and shout, "Johnson, sound-off!" Then you would hear this wonderful voice to start singing, "If I Only Had A Brain" from *The Wizard of Oz*. This never failed to crack up the Cadre and elicited responses such as, "Boy, he's got that right."

Two more of my BR's got this "special" treatment. One guy, Smith, had a fairly high-pitched voice, and the Cadre liked to place him in the front of the formation. The other guy, Jones, had a very deep, booming voice, and they would place him in the back of the formation. We would be marching merrily along, pressing up the hill of science as it were, when a corporal would shout, "Smith! Sound off!" To which Smith would reply, "Moo-moo! I'm a horny heifer!" Then another corporal would shout, "Jones! Sound off!" Jones would reply, "Moo-moo! I'm a raging bull!" This also always put the Cadre in stitches and had them shouting stuff like, "We've got to get these two together!"

(Footnote: I don't think anyone could get away with something like this these days. Do you?)

2

A Further Version of the Famous Bomb-Moving-Wall Story

Paul E. Johnson, '58

About the year 1956/57, we heard a muffled intense compression-like sound in the barracks one evening. Later, we learned that First Classman "Doc" Hardy was making a bomb and smoking a cigar at the same time. The powder ignited, blowing "Doc" out on the stoop and moving the wall a few inches into the adjoining room. The art teacher, "Suitcase" Simpson, who was walking towards his quarters about the same time, exclaimed, "Great, the Corps has gotten its balls back," and proceeded to organize some engineering majors to reposition the wall. It was several months before Col. Nichols figured out what happened and placed Doc on penalty tours.

Later that week, "Suitcase" handed me a drawing of a horse which I returned to him denying that it was mine. He returned with the drawing showing me where I had placed my name on it and loudly announced, "Johnson, you don't recognize your own crime."

3

A Salute to the Commandant

Jules M. "Bromo" Seletz, '53

Back in 1953, all major penalties were required to be answered in person to the Commandant. For reasons not to be mentioned here, I seemed to find myself in front of Colonel Pancake a number of times during my First Class year.

Along about the middle of the school year, I was once again disgruntled to stand before "Flapjack" and render him a slipshod, half-hearted, Terry-and-the-Pirates-type hand salute. He returned my salute with his usual grim facial expression.

That evening, at 1900 hours, the loudspeakers atop the sentry box in the courtyard of old barracks blared, "Attention! Attention in barracks! The entire Corps of Cadets will turn out in class uniform immediately and march into J.M. Hall. That is all."

When all 976 of us were squirming in our seats while grumbling about being forced to give up valuable time from study, sleep, card games or bull sessions, Colonel Pancake approached the podium on the stage in front of that famous Clinedinst painting of the charge up the hill of the Corps of Cadets at the 1864 Battle of New Market.

He announced, "Earlier today, I was chagrined to notice one of the sloppiest hand salutes in my entire military career. After tonight, I expect each of you to render only the smartest of hand salutes." Thankfully, he did not mention the offending cadet's name. The next thirty minutes, we were required to endure "Pancake's" imitation of all the wrong ways to salute, from the "two-finger from the eyebrow" to "the parachute drop."

As we exited J.M. Hall, I heard repeatedly from fellow cadets, "I'd sure like to get my hands on that damn cadet who's responsible for this."

Without looking about, this gross First-Class Private quietly slithered across the bricks, back into barracks, to return across the courtyard to the safety of Room 138.

4

Arrival

Strickler, Edmund R., '62

Ever since the fall of my junior year in high school, I wanted to attend VMI. At the time, Col. Lipscombe was head of admissions and had spoken at college night. The challenges he put forth appealed to me, and I was sold. Even though living at Virginia Beach, I had been born in Lexington and had many relatives in the area. I figured that there would be very few surprises. There were six of us who went to VMI that year from Princess Anne High School. Columbus Cartwright, Gene Wilson, John Spence and I had known each other since the 4th grade, and we thought we had the world by a string after graduating from high school.

In September 1958, my father and Columbus' father were taking John, Columbus and me to VMI for matriculation. When we left Virginia Beach, we were "full of ourselves" and couldn't wait to hit Lexington. Somewhere beyond Richmond, things began to quiet down and after Staunton there was silence. My father, in one of his great observations, said, "You guys certainly are quiet!" Yes, and we were scared. I can still remember that ride, and it turned out to be a ride to one of the greatest experiences of my life.

5

Attending a Fancy Dress Ball

W.D. Meola, '52

Washington and Lee University is in Lexington, Virginia, along with VMI, and every February sponsored a dance known throughout the area as the Fancy Dress Ball. The closest thing that could be compared to it at VMI was the Ring Figure in November. It is quite a formal event with Big Bands, evening gowns, tuxedos, and everything else that goes with such an affair. Every cadet I knew dreamed of going to this particular W&L dance. Getting there, however, took thoughtful and careful planning in order to avoid being *Out of Uniform* and *Absent Without Leave* (AWOL).

The honor code complicated planning but is evaded by devious maneuvering. An explanation of how personnel checks were made and how the honor code operates is in order. Every day one of the faculty or tactical (i.e., Tack) officers is put in charge of the barracks as Office in Charge or OC. One of the duties of the OC is to make a late night "stick check." Generally, this was after midnight and somewhere around 1 to 2 a.m. A stick check is simply the OC walking around each stoop (floor) and tapping each door on the stoop with a stick. He then records the time he tapped your door and if you are not "all right," the honor code requires you to be "boned" (penalized) for your infraction. I have forgotten what the penalty was for being AWOL, but if it wasn't dismissal, it was close to it.

Because you could not be "all right" at W&L, attending Fancy Dress Ball at stick check time, you would automatically change your status to AWOL unless avoidance measures were planned beforehand. It works this way. Knowledge that the OC starts his stick check on the fourth stoop and works his way down gives you the opportunity you need. You find a Rat (all Rats are on the fourth stoop) who is willing to get a few demerits and spend the night in your "sack" (i.e., cot) on the second stoop. After you return from the dance, you get in his sack. After the OC has "stick checked" his fourth stoop room (he is "all right" there), the rat then sneaks down to your room and gets in your "sack." When the OC stick checks your room, neither you nor the Rat are "all right," and your room must be reported, because there are two infractions.

The next morning you go to the Guardroom and find out what time the stick check was made. Some times there is no stick check. This is good—no one gets "boned." There almost always is, however, and the Rat gets three demerits for Visiting after Taps. As long as there is a single infraction reported that is all that is required. There were two potential problems associated with that though. 1) If the OC starts on the first stoop and works his way up, he would get to your room before the Rat could leave his room. Therefore, with only a single infraction, you are AWOL. Not a good scenario. 2) If the Officer of the Day (OD) asks, "Is that all?" you then have to report yourself AWOL. The OC, however, knows "how to play the game." He may have even gone to Fancy Dress Ball himself in the past, but as long as one infraction is reported, he is satisfied. These were the risks taken just to attend Fancy Dress Ball, but with the Glenn Miller Orchestra playing it seemed worth "Running the Block," an aphorism for going AWOL.

The stage is set to go to the dance, but the situation is still fraught with jeopardy. Not only do current cadets aspire to attend the dance; recent graduates serving as faculty often attend. Being seen and recognized by one of them is as bad as being caught by the stick check.

But I had my tuxedo, had arranged for the Rat to sleep in my sack, and off I went. I remember the band playing "St. Louis Blues March" and a trombone player playing his "brains out." I was blissfully unaware of the potential for disaster until I caught sight of Captain Lee Nichols. I did not have a date, which made me somewhat conspicuous. Listening to the music was how I enjoyed the dance. I must have been there for an hour or so when the band took a break. They spread out, went out for smokes, and to the refreshment stand for cokes. I was thirsty too and headed for the refreshment stand when coming around a corner I was met by Lee Nichols. I turned my head away at the last moment but I could not be sure he had not seen me. He taught one of the classes I had been in the year before and he knew me, if not my name, he certainly could recognize my face. I drank my coke and managed to stay away from Lee Nichols for the next dance set, but enjoying the dance now had lost its appeal. Rather than risk any more run-ins with Capt. Nichols I decided to leave, returned to barracks, and crawled into the Rat's sack. I had gone to Fancy Dressed Ball, enjoyed Glenn Miller's band for a while, and ran the risk of getting a major penalty. That was exciting enough.

Author's Note: Capt. Lee Nichols is still at the Institute, and I believe now is a Colonel heading up the Electrical Department. He has become a great favorite of the Class of '52 and certainly a favorite of myself. Although I can't be certain he did or did not see/recognize me at the dance, my intuition tells me he did and chose not to report me. This is possible, because he could not be sure. He was a tough disciplinarian and a taskmaster but in his dealing with cadets unfailingly fair.

6

Backfire

Josh Montero, '04

Last year (00-01) as a rat, I had this brilliant idea to play a joke on my roommate by sneaking a hot dog out of the mess hall, and putting it in the chamber of his rifle to see if the Cadre would do anything to him. Strictly as a joke, and also to make him clean his rifle. (This was after the ratline.) He saw it, but decided not to do anything about it. After a few days, I forgot about it and, sure enough, he turned it in at the end of the year with the hot dog still lodged in the barrel. When we returned as thirds, I had forgotten all about it, as did he, but the guy in the armory had cleaned the rifles over the summer, and guess what he had found. Your guess is much better than his, because he didn't have a clue! He called down the deputy commandant and told him that this was the worst he had ever seen in a rifle before.

Obviously, there is a lot of sodium in a hotdog and, as you know, salt and rust do not mix. The entire inside of the barrel had been corroded beyond repair and that was defacing institute property. They decided to give my rat roommate a special for "bouncing, banging, throwing rifle." He answered it upon his return and received twenty demerits, two weeks confinement, and thirty penalty tours. He just couldn't be happy with that and decided to tell the deputy commandant that his roommate was the one who put the hotdog in the rifle

So guess what, I got the same special except this time it also said, "Putting hotdog in chamber of rifle." The report actually said the word hotdog. It was so funny. I was kind of nervous but my roommates thought it was hilarious. (We already knew it was coming because the BR that owned the rifle told me.) The penalty for that is a number five which is thirty demerits, six weeks confinement, and thirty penalty tours, plus loss of rank. All of my BR's that knew about it seriously thought he would rip my head off upon answering the special so they wanted to hear all of it. Not hear all about it, they wanted to hear it. So they talked me into wearing a handheld tape recorder under my gray blouse and recording our nice conversation.

Man he gripped me out pretty bad. I answered him, "Yes sir, this rat…" I called myself a rat. How pathetic is that? Well, by the time I got up to my room, there was an audience waiting to hear the recording. I played it, and they all laughed at me. Honestly, I thought it was pretty funny too. I ended up keeping my rank, getting twenty demerits, and twenty-five penalty tours, ten of which had to be spent in the armory cleaning rifles (that's 600 minutes of cleaning rifles!!!!), and three weeks confinement. I also made a copy of the special with the word "hotdog," and I am going to try and get it in the Bomb under, "outrageous specials."

7

B. Davis Mayo, Professor of Math

W.D. Meola, '52

Any cadet who was fortunate enough to have had BD Mayo for Calculus probably has heard of, or told, the many stories that have circulated VMI for ages. BD had the kind of personality that one remembers, particularly by this one, who relied heavily upon BD's cadet/teacher explanation of how to pass Calculus. There are many stories about BD. Here are three of them: 1) How to Pass Calculus, 2) Closing the Transom, and 3) Class Dismissed.

How to Pass Calculus

It may not have been the first day of Calculus, but it wasn't too long after the year began when I believe BD got the feeling that we weren't getting what he was teaching. I do not know how many of Section 3C (math Section 5) had any pre-Calculus instruction, but I knew I was in for a rough time. I pulled out my old Calculus book and found these names in Section 3C: JB Hyatt, WD Kearney, WK Lederman, RD Leighty, RG Long, TL Lyne, JW MacDonald, HC Magee, JL Martin, MR Mays, JR McCarthy, W.D. Meola, JP Miller, GA Moning, H Nanninga and RL Lambert who was the section leader. Martin later wore a gold star and was our class brain; the rest of us were at Calculus's mercy.

Back to the story. BD went to the board and drew a "stick" figure of a cadet and another stick figure of himself. He then drew a line between the two stick figures as if they were carrying a telephone pole or something and labeled it Calculus. Stick Figure Cadet was walking to the left and Stick Figure Teacher was walking along behind. Together they were carrying Calculus. Then BD drew two more stick figures both facing the same way and drew another line between the two but this time Stick Figure Teacher had dropped his end of Calculus. Now BD drew a third set of stick figures still facing the same way and again drew a line between the two only this time Stick Figure Cadet had dropped his end of Calculus.

Then BD explained: In the first set of stick figures Cadet and Teacher are carrying Calculus together and, as long as that continued, there was no way in Hell Cadet would flunk Calculus. In the second set of stick figures, Teacher had dropped his end of Calculus whereas Cadet had continued to hold on to his end. BD explained that although it would be tougher, Cadet could continue to pull his way to the end of the school year and pass Calculus. Then BD pointed to the third set of stick figures where Cadet had dropped his end of Calculus. Everyone in the class now became aware of what was going to happen, and BD explained that no matter how hard Teacher pushed, there was no way in Hell Cadet could pass Calculus if he dropped his end.

I remembered that little scenario and although I was not a brilliant student, in fact, maybe a little backward in this upper math, I needed a 6 on my final exam in order to pass Calculus for the year. At that time VMI graded on the basis of 10 with six passing, and even though you had a perfect 10 throughout the year you still had to make at least a 5 on your final. When the grades were posted, it attracted a large gathering and when someone told me the grades for Calculus were posted, I became one of the assembled. I couldn't see the grade sheet so I hollered, "What did Meola get," and held my breath. Someone said, "Who" and I said back, "Meola! Meola, WD!" Then the reply, "Meola got a 6." I had passed Calculus.

Closing the Transom

The classroom had windows to our left and blackboard in front and to our right. I don't remember what was in the rear of the room but the door was also on the right and somewhere near the front of the room. In the summer the windows could be opened along with the transom so a nice cross breeze could pass through the room. That was air conditioning late 1940's style.

BD would then explain a problem or go over the text we had been assigned to read and fielded questions. We all hoped that we could keep BD so busy that he would forget to send us to the board. Some days it worked; however, in retrospect I think he knew all along when we weren't going to the board and just liked to keep us guessing. On most days however, everyone went to the board and we were given two problems, alternating 1 and 2 so that the problem either side of you was the "other" problem. This was done to protect us from cheating and from the Honor Court. If the adjacent problems were the same as yours they are too easy to see even when you really aren't trying to see.

After you had finished struggling with your problem and went back to your seat, BD would go over it with a long pointed stick. Sometimes struggle was too tame a word so BD would sit you down even though you weren't done. Then he would come to my work. I usually had only slight knowledge of how the problem should have been solved and my work generally showed it although I tried to cover all of my board with chalk so it looked good. BD looked at my work and took a step or two back then looked at it again. Then he turned to me and the class. At some point I always knew we were in for one of BD's explanations and this was going to be it. I tried to look inquisitively at him to show I really wanted to know how to do that problem but I knew an explanation was forthcoming.

BD said, "Do you all see that transom there over the door?" and we all looked toward the transom. Boy, I thought to myself, this is going to be good. And he went on, "Do you all see that metal rod attached to the transom?" Some of us audibly said "un uh" and some of us just nodded. BD continued, "There are two ways to close that transom. Most people would walk to the door and push the rod up until the transom was closed and sit back down. Then there's the other way. Some of you would rather swing by your asshole on the doorknob and kick it closed with your heels." It became painfully obvious he was referring to my convoluted board work when he said, "Now Meola, find a pitch fork and get that stuff BS off the board."

Class Dismissed

Now this story is not one where I was present, however the people who related it to me practically certified to its authenticity. At VMI, certifying means it is fact or true. I believe this happened to one of the third class sections that were a year ahead of us. They could not have been taking Calculus at the same time that we were so maybe it was a differential equations class. No matter, this is how it goes.

Each section has a Section Leader. In the above story "How to Pass Calculus" RL Lambert was our Section Leader. The Section Leader's task is pretty simple, the class lines up, and the Section Leader calls the roll and notes who's absent, who's on leave, or sick, marches the section to class, salutes the instructor while the class is at attention, and then reports to the instructor. The instructor then can note in his records absent and missing individuals that later can have a bearing on that individual's grade. Sometimes athletes are away from the campus and may miss a test so the instructor will want to make sure the athlete makes-up the test.

The instructor, in this case BD, generally will say something like "at ease" and the class will sit down. In all the math classes I had, in so far as I can remember, we had small tables to sit at. I cannot remember if there were more than one cadet to a table they were that small. At any rate, class was under way and the Section Leader having done his duty also sat down. He happened to be in the very front of the room so he could better perform his duty directly with BD. To some cadets math was an abhorrence that had to be suffered; otherwise you could not advance to the next level. As such, math became extremely boring. Unfortunately this Section Leader was one of those cadets who was bored and although right under the nose of the BD, he fell asleep. BD finally turned away from the blackboard where he had been explaining a problem and noted the dozing cadet. Without altering his lecture or modifying his voice in anyway whatsoever BD walked up to the Section Leaders desk and using the long point stick mentioned earlier slammed the broad side of the pointer flat across the desk and quite near to the Section Leader's head. The Section Leader snapped to attention and hollered, "Class dismissed." The class had a great time laughing at the section leader and so did BD. The penalty could have been a 10-2-10 (ten demerits, two weeks confinement and ten penalty tours). BD did not report the Section Leader, but suffice to say Section Leader never again fell asleep in one of BD's classes.

8

Clean What?

Houston H. (Tex) Carr, '59

Remember this? During our four years at The Institute, we had, as I remember, three Commandants and, of course, four First Captains. During our Second Class year (Fall 1957), we had parade, as usual, on a Friday. It rained before and during the parade, making the Hill a bit messy. By the time The Corps returned to barracks they had wet and muddy straight pants. Our First Captain, Jim West '58, walked into the Commandant's Office, with a pair of wet and muddy grey straight pants in hand, and asked in a very straight forward manner, "Who is going to clean the Corps uniforms?" Not sure of the outcome, but Jim took up for us without hesitation.

9

Corps Trip

Lance Pickering, '88

In my rat year, our corps trip was to the Oyster Bowl in Norfolk for what turned out to be the final VMI/VA Tech football game. I traveled to the game with my dykes. When we got to Norfolk on Saturday, my dykes decided I would be in charge of smuggling our liquid refreshments into the game. Being a rat, I didn't feel I had any cause to object. So, they placed two pints of Virginia Gentleman under my blouse, and one pint up my left sleeve. The right sleeve was left empty so I could salute. Nice of them to think of that, huh?

Needless to say, I was very nervous carrying around all that booze under my blouse. But I was a rat, and my dykes had given me an order. As we were forming up for our march-on, a rumor started circulating that the Tech Corps was going to try to disrupt our march-on. As the rumor started to make the rounds, our Cadre started to tell us rats that if the rumor proved true, they'd better see blood on all of our gloves.

Now I became very concerned. How was I going to fight and uphold the honor of VMI with three bottles of Virginia Gentleman in my blouse? As I was pondering my predicament, a corporal noticed my apprehension and approached me saying, "Pickering, what's your problem? Are you afraid to fight?"

Now, I was really sweating. I couldn't decide what to do or say. I mean, should I try and bluff my way out of the situation, or should I fess up and risk getting boned for having alcohol in ranks. Finally, I decided honesty was my best recourse, and I said, "No sir! I'm not afraid to fight, but I do have a problem." Then I showed him what was under my blouse. The corporal looked up at me, looked at the bottle again, then looked up at me again and grinned. I thought, "Oh boy! I'm dead!" Then he yelled, "O.K., Rats! New plan. If the Hokies attack, surround Pickering! At all costs protect Pickering!" Then he whispered into my ear, "I'll expect a drink when we get inside." To which I gave a hearty, "Yes sir!"

In the end, the Hokies did not try to disrupt our march-on, and I found a new friend in the third class.

10

A Cow on the Barracks Roof?

George A. Ford, '54

While I didn't actually witness this myself, it was told to me by two Brother Rats and a '53 who attended Summer School after our Rat Year. They swore it was true, and others confirmed it. It seems that Summer School was a pretty relaxed place at VMI, and, of course, there was no guard team on duty, so this story is believable.

It seems like five guys, one '53, two 52's, and two of our BR's were out partying late one night and got very creative. Someone remembered a cow tethered in the front yard of one of the small houses down the hill behind the Mess Hall and the Hospital. After a short brainstorming session, someone came up with the idea of: wouldn't it be neat if we could get that cow up on the barracks roof? So they tromped down to the cow's yard to check things out. Sure enough, the cow was tied to a stake in the ground with a rope, in a place where taking it was unlikely to be seen. Fortunately, or unfortunately, depending on how you look at the situation, they realized that this brazen task might take some planning and agreed to postpone any further action and to meet for lunch the next day.

Well, planning proceeded the next day, and that night after midnight they did the deed. After untying the cow, they led her behind the mess hall, then the old hospital and the chemistry building along sloping hillsides over the "Nile" to the door to a trash room on the lower (main sinks) level of barracks. Coaxing the cow to walk up the stairs out of the main sinks to the courtyard apparently took over an hour.

After the first stairs, the cow had learned to climb, and the chore became easier. So, they took her up the stairs in the northeast corner of old barracks to the fourth stoop. The noise awoke a few sightseers and more helpers, so by the time they had led, pushed and pulled the cow around the fourth stoop to the center of the West side, there were more than a dozen herders and several puddles and pods on the stoops. The herders were getting their share of splashes and splatters on them. You may recall that in the middle of the West side of the fourth stoop, there was a door to a narrow stairway leading to what was referred to as the fifth stoop. There were only two rooms up there in a structure perched on the roof. Groups like the "Cadet" paper, and the General Committee used them.

The cow became obstinate at the narrow stairway. But, undaunted, the valiant Summer Cadets pushed, pulled and tugged the cow up the stairs. Then, somehow they got her out of a low window onto the roof by removing the upper part of the window, and lifting the cow's feet out one at a time. They were thoughtful enough to tie the cow, and leave a bucket of water, and some food.

It was apparently about ten the next morning before an assistant commandant heard the mooing, of the cow needing milking, on the roof and went to investigate. Of course, he found the cow, water, food, and a number of nice cow pods and puddles.

If you think that's funny, wait till you hear about getting the cow down. First some local farmers were summoned to lead the cow down the stairs. They got the cow back through the window into the small upper room, but there was no way that cow was going to go down those narrow stairs. So, they took the cow back out on to the roof where it had to be fed and watered and cleaned up after for four more days. The cow's owner showed up that afternoon and stood on the roof alternately cursing everything VMI, and hugging and kissing his cow. By then, a large crowd of not only the VMI family, but Minks, Lexingtonians and visitors had gathered on the west side of Barracks thoroughly enjoying the excitement.

After a day or so, they ended up getting a contractor to build a huge A-frame like structure that projected out over the front of barracks. The inboard end of the structure had to be weighed down with sandbags that exceeded the weight of the cow. The fifty-pound bags of sand, of course, had to be individually lugged up five flights of stairs, and later back down again. Finally, the cow was hung in a sling, hoisted over the wall, and lowered, bellowing at the top of her tranquilized lungs, to the grass on the west side of barracks, right behind Stonewall Jackson and his battery of cannons. The gathered crowd cheered and cheered as the cow's feet touched the ground.

Apparently, there wasn't any effort to find the perpetrators. The cow apparently had no long-term ill affects. The roof was cleaned, and the administration must have laughed as much as I do every time I think of this story. We could call it one of the Legends or myths of the Class of 1954, so it doesn't matter if it is true or not; it's just funny.

11

Cunning and Desperate

Erwin Hanke, '71

It was early spring of my First Class year. The Rats ('scuse me, Fourth Classmen at that point) were happy just being out of the ratline. The Thirds were anticipating moving up in the world by moving down a stoop, soon to be weighed down by those round anchors called "class rings." The Class of '72 was looking forward to being in charge of barracks, finally showing "Puzzle Palace" how it should and could be run. My class wasn't as solidified into a singleness of purpose as our younger brothers, because we were staring into the cold, hard eyes of the Real World. Some of us we looking to graduate school. Some to marriage. Some to joining the family business, or any business. Some to being unemployed. Some to being anywhere other than the VMI. Many were looking to go on active duty, some immediately, some delayed. "Active duty" in those days looked like the 'Nam. "I want to be an Airborne Ranger. Live my life in constant danger. I want to go to Viet-Nam…left, right, left." I don't remember Tricky Dick having started any de-escalation at that point. The Class of '71, however, had to remain focused enough to get through Finals (and I'm not talking just about the Hops and parties).

By this stage of the game, we all had our personal, tried and true methods of dealing with studying in general and exams in particular. Some studied in the academic buildings. Some lucky sons had study carrels within the enforced quiet of Preston Library. Some studied alone, others in groups. My roommate of four years, Andy Yurchak (first-ranking EE in our class), would look at his books while wearing headphones with music blaring. After about twenty minutes, he would look up at me from across our facing desks; a wide grin would cross his face as he slowly closed his books. He would take off the headphones, turn off the record player, and then dive onto his hay or a couple of comforters (depending upon his status and the time of day/night). You would have thought that he was a liberal artist! I think our other roommate, Craig (the Dog) Beigel, had some special permit to study in W&L's law library or an apartment above Pres Brown's. (Good grief, that man could run some "stuff" past the Commandant's office! He could play a permit like Meade Stith could play a guitar.)

Like Andy, I studied in our room. Good old Club 172. Andy, I, and this year, Craig, were the happy occupants of this most outstanding of barracks' abodes. In each of the three years since we had had the privilege of choosing our own room and roommates, Andy had won us the X72 room in that part of New Barracks that we referred to as "the Grotto." We had selected these rooms next to the trash chute for the powerful symbolism, convenient location (not always a good thing, but great just before room inspection) and for their unusual semi-triangular shape due to their position near the sally port on the backside turn of the 1949 addition. The down side was that our doorway was a favorite haunt of several TAC's, because the position afforded them a sweeping view of New Barracks as well as the west side stoop of Old Barracks. During the final exam period of 1971, I discovered another down side to this otherwise very tony piece of real estate.

Most people acquainted with Lexington know that VMI, while the best institution of higher learning in town, is not the only college in town. Fewer people might be aware that W&L also had ROTC. Many of those "cadets" apparently had a different exam schedule than us Keydets, and those "cadets" had apparently procured permission to utilize the VMI outdoor rifle range over the period of our final exams. I'm certain this was another dastardly mink plot to sabotage our GPA's rather than an innocent attempt to improve their marksmanship. Those who might have known and were in a position to allow or disallow this occupation for that bullet-riddled parcel of flint and mud situated directly across the "Nile" from where I was cramming for all I was worth probably gave no thought to my study habits or my sensitivities to having the report of round after round randomly reverberating around my room. I prefer to believe that the Administration was an unthinking dupe rather than a co-conspirator of those "frat" boys. Little comfort in that.

I suffered through this reenactment of the battle of Droop Mountain all Monday, in the unfounded hope that this was a one-day event. Doomed to disappointment, I tried earphones and cotton balls on Tuesday. I appealed to the Authorities, but was told that the permit was approved; those noble souls had to prepare themselves for the Indiantown Gap experience; so I was S.O.L. But I was VMI-trained, keen of intellect, cunning and desperate...a force to be reckoned with...and...I had a plan.

Maybe it was the pressure of the final Finals, maybe the lack of sleep, or possibly the product of the nervous energy that causes ulcers in some and irrational acts in others. Maybe it was the pent-up need to perform some last silly, stupid, ill advised, juvenile act before I left VMI (it wasn't). Certainly the perceived need for study in barracks as I had grown accustomed to it was a factor. That's my explanation. Hey, this was for the good of the corps! I wasn't the only one studying for his life on the backside of barracks! In those days, if you flunked out, the notice from your draft board arrived home before you did. So this had to be done, and it was a one-man job. No need to involve Brother Rats in this daring deed. If I go down, I go down alone. (Those could have been the bywords of my cadetship instead of "You don't need a Weatherman to know which way the wind blows." Double entendre all around.)

My plan was simple. Man, was it simple. Like everyone in the corps, I had spent time on the rifle range. We're talking "live fire" here, Comrade. Conditions must be met. Procedure must be followed. "Ready on the right…Ready on the left…Ready on the firing line…Commence firing!" The red range flag had to be hoisted high above the hillside to show windage and to, literally, indicate to all "within range" that live fire was taking place. If that flag couldn't be flown, they couldn't shoot. No shooting, no noise. No noise, normal study. Normal study, Dean's List. Graduation. Life would be good. That's the mission…Eliminate the flag.

At first light Wednesday morning, I was up before the chickens, way before Bill the Bugler. I donned my BDU's, snuck out of barracks, crossed the "Nile," and maneuvered up to the rifle range shed. It was locked with a chain, but there was a gap between the doors, a gap wide enough to allow a skinny, sweaty young fool to slip through. Squeezed in. Find the red flag! Got it! And back out I slipped. Furtive glances left and right. No campus police, no MP's, no federal agents. Wiped out my size 10R boot tracks. Don't want Forensics to catch me that easily. Sure to be a countywide search.

Now, to get rid of the evidence. Can't keep it or even trash it. Honor Court. So on to Phase 2 of the plan. Across Post to Alumni Field. What better place to hide a flag than up a flag pole, so I ran it up the pole on the right of the far, corps side, where on game days the school flags of the Southern Conference always flew. That day there was only one, the flag of Fool(ed) U. There it hid in plain sight. There was no firing on the range that day, or the rest of the week. Mission accomplished!

You don't suppose that they were only using the range for two days anyway, do you?

12

Do You See What I See?

Houston H. (Tex) Carr, '59

My dad, uncle, and brother attended W&L. I, seeing the light, came to VMI. Well, I wanted engineering and W&L was a liberal arts school, you know, where history majors go to study. My Dad told me there was a more heated rivalry in the olden days. For example, once there was a riff and someone painted or wrapped the columns on the W&L colonnade with red, white, and yellow stripes. Remember that the colonnade is several buildings long, so this must have been a sight to behold.

13

Double Trouble

RB Lane, '75

I have two brother rats who are identical twins, Barry and Larry Lineback. When I say identical, I mean identical. I roomed with Larry for two years and it took me awhile to learn to tell them apart.

During our first class year Larry would wait for a rat to come along and head up one of the stairways in barracks. He'd get up in the rat's face, flame him a bit, and challenge him to a race up the stairs to the third or fourth stoop. If the rat won the race, Larry would let him out of the ratline for the day, or something to that affect. Larry and the rat would get side by side at the bottom of the steps and they would begin the race. Larry would purposely fall behind and visions of victory and a day free of the ratline would begin to form in the rat's mind. If course, and unbeknownst to the rat, Barry was waiting for him at the top of the steps. The look on the rat's face upon seeing his competition at the top of the steps waiting for him was priceless.

14

Drinking Privileges

David Schwab, '73

I don't remember the exact date, but it was about the middle of the second semester in 1970. General Shell, the Superintendent, granted permission to the Rat class of 1973 to drink alcohol, within the limits of state law, of course. My Brother Rats were ecstatic; I didn't care one way or the other, and I figured this proclamation would have no effect on my daily routine.

I was wrong.

Two of my three roommates in room 454 couldn't wait to head for *Jonnies* and the *College Inn* during RQ on that first Saturday. I think I did some studying, watched some TV, and hung around the PX. My roommates returned just in time for CCQ, one of them carrying the other. The three of us who were able to stand got Brother Rat into his hay and settled in as the lights went out.

It seems to me it was about an hour or so later that we all awoke to the telltale smell of beer and vomit. Brother Rat had hurled his evening's liquid sustenance all over his hay and the floor.

While the other two took him to the sinks at the sally port for a good scrubbing, I was detailed to clean up the mess. Fortunately for us, the Corporal of the Guard bought my story when he investigated the lights on in our room. We got Brother Rat back into bed, and the rest of the night passed without incident.

15

Fireworks Run in the Family

George A. Ford, Jr., '54

This story is about two incidents with fireworks during our Rat year. But, in a larger sense, it is about a Rat's need to "get back at authority." What better way to annoy the hierarchy than to blow up a firecracker in barracks and not get caught? Speaking of getting caught, I must have had an angel looking over me for not getting caught shooting hundreds of firecrackers during our rat year. If I had been caught, I probably would have walked penalty tours all year instead of just two months.

The first incident was at Parents' Weekend, which, if I recollect correctly, was the weekend VMI beat Georgia Tech, and we were out of the Ratline for the weekend. About 10:30 Saturday night, I was loafing in my Dyke's room with two of the three First classmen who lived there, and a couple of Brother Rats who also dyked in the room. I think it was Room 206, on the Washington Arch side of barracks, second stoop, close to the stairway in the southwest corner.

We heard these loud POP—POP—POP, on and on and on. We rushed out on the stoop, and colored balls of fire were flying through the air. There was a whole line of Roman Candles stuck in the ground between the sentinel box in the center of the courtyard and the entrance to Washington Arch, with this roly-poly old gentleman lighting them. The sentinel was running in from New Barracks yelling, "Corporal of the Guard! Corporal of the Guard! Corporal of the Guard! Sir, Sir, you can't do that! Stop! Stop! Please Stop!"

The gentleman was my dad, chuckling in his cups, and lighting another Roman candle. I started yelling, "Dad, Dad, you can't do that, get the hell out of here."

He just laughed and waved up at me.

Fortunately, the Officer of the Guard, who arrived on the scene without the Officer of the Day, or the Tactical Officer in Charge, was an easygoing first class private. Nick was also my dyke's roommate. Thank God for small favors. He stood there, let my Dad light the last Roman candle, then took him by the arm and escorted him to his car and sent him on his way. No repercussions. I was afraid for weeks afterward that it would come back to haunt me. Well, I was in a bunch of trouble, but never attributed it to my Dad's celebration of a VMI victory.

When Dad and my stepmother and sister left on Sunday, he slipped me a package with ten packs of 100 one and a half-inch Chinese Firecrackers strung together.

Most of these one hundred packs were unwound into single firecrackers that were tossed out the back window of new barracks, into the courtyard, or shoved through the heat pipe hole in the wall into Al Burton and Ed Garbee's room next door where they would go off unexpectedly. For a while, they thought someone was throwing them in the window. Al and Ed and I roomed together for our last three years. They were amazingly tolerant of my rat year antics, and I still wonder if they took me in as a roommate in self-defense.

But, my real masterpiece was after Christmas. My two first semester roommates had left school. I moved to the West side of the fourth stoop in the last room before new barracks with Don Ferry, Phil Cancellere, and a '53 Bull Rat who eventually left about twenty minutes ahead of the Honor Court coming to try him for something. We never found out what.

It was cold as holy hell one January night, and since it was early in the semester, there was no need to study. So, what trouble could we think up? There was one string of 100 firecrackers left. I don't remember who thought of this, but dumb me carried it out. Directly across the courtyard from our room was an empty room. How could we get those firecrackers to go off in the empty room so we could watch the guard team and the upperclassmen scramble to find out what happened and who did it?

I wrapped up in coveralls, long underwear, ski jacket hat etc. We scotch taped a lighted Lucky Strike cigarette to the fuse end of the string of firecrackers so the cigarette would burn down to eventually light the fuses. We folded the string of firecrackers longwise in a Life Magazine, and I tucked it under my left armpit. It was about a half-hour before taps, and the cold stoops were empty. I calmly, but scared to death, walked the rat line down the North wall of old barracks, around the corner, and up to the door to the empty room on the East side. I opened the door, placed the Life Magazine with the firecrackers in it on the floor, and left the door slightly ajar so the noise would come out of the room louder. Turning around, I walked the Rat Line back to our room unable to contain myself from laughing out loud. My three roommates were of course at the door watching, but as far as I know no one else suspected anything.

We stood looking out of the door windows for what seemed forever, believing that the cigarette must have gone out. Finally, Blam, Blam, Boom, Boom, Boom, BANG, BANG…a hundred times. The room lit up like daylight, and the smoke was so thick, you couldn't see in.

Everyone in old barracks came to see. Brother Rats to the doors (we weren't allowed to loiter on the stoop) and upperclassmen out on the stoops. Some upperclassmen came up to the room, and the whole Guard Team came running. The Officer of the Day had his saber drawn. When he went in the room and turned on the light, the smoke was so thick one could see nothing. Soon they got the windows open. The smoke cleared revealing a billion little bits of Chinese firecracker papers.

Remember the time, 1951. There was a lot of fear of Russia. Some initially thought it was a Russian attack. When word went out that it was firecrackers, everyone but the guard team, and the Commandant, who had come over to see what was happening, thought it was funny. The guard team conducted a room-to-room search. They questioned everyone in all the rooms on the East side of the fourth and third stoops, and they went halfway down the North and South Sides. Apparently it never occurred to them that someone could have done it from all the way across the courtyard.

It was a couple of hours after Taps when they finished the witch-hunt; cleaned all the papers out of the empty room, and turned out the light. The four of us had tears in our eyes and pains in our ribs from laughing. Needless to say, we kept our mouths shut for a few months until the furor died down. I thought I was courageous at the time. Now, it seems like a pretty stupid thing to have done. But, I'm glad we did it, because we will go to our graves laughing about it.

16

First # 1

Pickering, Lance

(Author's note: I don't mention any other names in this story, because the other parties might not want their involvement in this episode known publicly.)

During Ring Figure weekend, each class gets to assume the class privileges of the class above them. Except, of course, the rats. They're still rats. As part of this, second classmen get a dyke for the weekend known as their ring figure dyke.

During my rat year, my ring figure dykes decided they were going to have a little celebration up on the rappelling cliffs on Thursday night after they had received their rings. They informed me that my attendance at this little soiree was desired and required. Now, as a rat, it would never occur to me to say no to a request from an upperclassman unless involved breaking the Honor Code. So, I joined the party on the rappelling cliffs. We ended up having a grand time and consumed great quantities of adult beverages.

As taps approached, we headed back to barracks. However, my ring figure dykes decided we were having too much fun to let a little thing like taps get in the way of the party. So, they decided to continue the party in their room, and once again I was told that my presence was required. In fact, one of my ring figure dykes said that if I wasn't in their room after the stick ran he would come up to my room and beat the tar out of me.

We got back to barracks and slipped through a first classman's window. When we got into the first's room, I got a surprise. There was a sweat party going on in the old courtyard! Now, being a good BR, I was determined that I wasn't going to let my BR's go through a sweat party while I watched. Fortunately, the first classman was of sounder mind, and he convinced me that it would be an extraordinarily bad idea if I joined the sweat party. So, we waited until the sweat party was over, and I slipped into the crowd heading for the fourth stoop. I made it back to my room without incident and waited for the stick to run so I could rejoin my ring figure dykes or incur their wrath.

When I got down to my ring figure dyke's room, I found that two of them had passed out. However, this did not deter the other two from wanting to continue the party. I also learned that they had dropped one half-gallon bottle of whiskey on their floor when they were using their bed straps to haul the bottles up to their room. This fact would turn out to be our downfall. As we were talking and having fun, I looked up and saw a figure in the doorway with his hand on the light switch. As my heart came up in my throat, the light came on, and there stood the Tac. It turned out we were being a bit loud and had attracted his attention. When he got to the room, he quickly smelled the Virginia Gentleman and just as quickly ascertained what was going on in the room. He took our names, except for the guys who had passed out, and sent me back to my room. Not a great start to my ring figure dykes' Ring Figure.

That is not the end of the story though. While my ring figure dykes quickly got specials and number 1's (15 demerits, 4 months barracks confinement, and 60 PT's), I had to cool my heels for a while waiting for the hammer to fall. It seems that since I was a rat there was some debate about what to do with me. The powers that be couldn't decide whether they should bone me or give me to the RDC. I learned of this because one of my dykes was RDC. Honestly, I couldn't decide which fate I preferred. They were equally bad. In the end, they decided to bone me, and I gained the dubious distinction of being the first member of my class to get a number 1. Before my time at VMI was up, I acquired the equally dubious "honor" of receiving the most number ones of any cadet and still graduate. In the end, I had 4 number ones—but those are other stories.

17

Football

Sam E. Woolwine, '58

My story is about the 1957 football team, our third class year. We won our 9th game, beating the citadel down there 14-13. The next game with VA Tech, we got beat 45 to nothing, finishing the season 1 and 9. The next year, we were 3.6 and 1. That summer, we had to go to summer camp. Lou Farmer and I made the trip to Ft. Mead together and had plenty of time to talk about what we could do as co-captains to turn this team around. We decided, with coach McKenna's enthusiastic support, to write every team member a letter of encouragement: that we had the talent but were lacking the commitment that it takes to have a winning team. Everyone took it personally, and when we gathered for early practice in August, it was so obvious that everyone was willing to make the commitment regardless of what price it took to get it done, as Paul Harvey says. Now the rest of the story: Everyone knows we were 9-0 and 1, tying Holy Cross in Worchester, Massachusetts 21-21. Our third game of the season, we finished the season defeating VA tech 14-6 in Roanoke, on Thanksgiving Day, to remain undefeated. The Class of 1958 is awfully proud of all of our classmates who were part of this team.

18

Greasy Bird

Erwin Hanke, '71

I must begin by advising the reader that this event took place in 1967, and thirty years after the fact, when recounted to the principal player during an evening of libations in Moody Hall, he admitted no memory of the event, though he did not deny it either.

Back in the days when we held parades on the "parade ground," not a "parade deck" (a deck is on a ship, not a hill, isn't it?), those fortunate enough to have to march down for Saturday DRC occasionally got to enjoy Southern fried chicken ala Club Crozet, aka "Greasy Bird." As rats, we had no real alternative to the experience. We little ratties were assigned seating by company (E Company, Sir! Best d*mned company on the Hill, Sir!), nine to a table, plus a First Classman to guide us in learning all of the niceties and nuances of dining "family style." As the corps ate basically all at one time, the tables and chairs were necessarily very close. The significance of this fact will become evident in a moment.

On this particular evening, I had the good fortune to be the last rat to arrive at the table, and so had the privilege of assuming the chair of honor, next to the serving island situated between the four tables assigned to our cadet waiter. It was my responsibility to insure that my table received *at least* one quarter of everything delivered thereto. Immediately to my left, at the table's head, sat our reigning First, Mr. Dick Wise. I'm not sure why our happy little table was getting to enjoy the tutorage of Mr. Wise, a FCP, rather than a ranker. Could be he had lost a bet, or just agreed to help out a BR that Saturday night, because he was on confinement anyway. In any event, there we all were.

As the rat server, I was busy pulling everything onto our table ASAP, dumping as necessary to return the dishes to the island for refills. All of this was taking place while the rest of the corps was filing into the mess hall. Once all were in, the regimental commander would call the corps to attention for the saying of "grace." Even back in 1967, way ahead of his time, Mr. Wise did not feel compelled to delay the enjoyment of his repast for those slower than he, so he politely asked me to serve him the main course, the platter of "greasy bird." While keeping my chin well inside the top of my blouse collar, I picked up the plate before me and offered it to my left.

"No, mouse. You serve from the left!" he said. I didn't understand, evident from the glazed, rolling-eyed look I assumed. "No, rattie. Get up and serve me from my left!" Oh, I got it! Mr. Wise was extending me his First Class privilege of "walking in the mess hall" to serve him the chicken from around his other side.

I pushed my seat back, got up, and started to race around the table with the platter of "bird." About the time I had made it three-fifths of the way, the RC called the corps to attention. The foot-and-one-half aisle through which I was running evaporated as my BR's all pushed out their chairs to stand at attention. I went flying, the platter went flying, and the chicken got to relive the experience as well.

Dick Wise, first class pagan that he was at that time, had remained seated, so he simply reached down to pick up a piece that had made it to the last turn. "Thanks, rat," he said, as he bit into the bird.

19

High Explosives

Tony Lash, '58

In the grand VMI tradition of high explosive detonations, my roomie Ron Culver's fervid imagination produced the *piece de resistance* of our cadetship and, I believe, the Twentieth Century. He obtained fifty-eight 2 ½" diameter ground based aerial bombs, mounted them on plywood, and connected the fuses in a series-parallel configuration. At about 01:00, on a winter morning, he set the infernal device in the new barracks courtyard and lit the fuse. A few of the bombs launched their missiles singly at short intervals. The range was perfect—they exploded just above the fourth stoop. After about eight explosions, the bombs began to go off simultaneously and in a staccato sequence. It truly sounded like World War III had begun at VMI, particularly in the early morning stillness.

The fusillade went on for some seven minutes and woke up at least half of Lexington. Alex and I could be heard cheering on the tape recording we made, and also some imprecations from other cadets who didn't appreciate such a magnificent spectacle. I shall never forget the sight of the poor rat sentinel standing at port arms about fifteen yards from the spectacle, in rapt astonishment and complete helplessness. The sergeant of the guard retrieved the smoking debris when all was still and left it in the commandant's office. I was the editor of the VMI Cadet at the time. In the next issue a picture of the explosive array before it was set off appeared. The administration didn't bother to ask how it came into my possession.

20

Horizontal Lab

Houston H. (Tex) Carr, '59

Engineering was, to say the least, a bit different than the liberal arts as far as curriculum. It was, also, more dangerous. The Civil Engineers would march to class once a year, carrying a six-foot slide rule. Not sure if it was due to the eyesight of the professor or that CE's just liked very large toys. The electrical engineers played around with dangerous voltages all the time. We had afternoon labs generally twice a week, where we would turn on motors, run generators, and hitch up transformers. I remember one such occasion when we were using a constant current transformer, the kind they used on street lighting. I brushed the output with the back of my hand and was moved a little ways back. The output carried 600 volts, and it was enough to get your attention. Because of these fun-and-games we played, the EE's were required to re-certify in what would now be called CPR. We would, thus, have horizontal lab each semester. You could tell which day it was because the EE's would line up in class ranks with blankets under arm. We used these in artificial respiration drill, but the LA's thought they were for sleeping, possibly because they used blankets at LA Beach.

21

How the Institute Got Buzzed

Tom Colvin, '53

In 1973, I was, as a Lieutenant Colonel, the commander of the 309th Tactical Fighter Squadron, the "Blue Ducks," stationed at Homestead AFB, Florida. We flew F-4E "Phantom II" aircraft, at the time the most advanced fighter in USAF service.

A fortuitous fact was that my Wing Commander (Commander, 31st Tactical Fighter Wing) was Colonel Alonzo J. Walter, Jr., VMI 1949B. Lon Walter was (and is) a staunch supporter of the Institute.

One of the four Flight Commanders working for me in my squadron was Major Howard T. Moss, VMI 1960. Howard was from Richmond, and his parents still lived there. We had a few other VMI graduates in the 31st TFW, but that is gratuitous to this story.

I wanted to go to our 20th reunion.

I went to Col. Walter and asked for permission for a "weekend navigational training flight" with the implied goal of going to my 20th reunion. Such flights were legal and not infrequently done. Col. Walter wanted to know where I would land, and I told him Byrd Field (full name: Richard Evelyn Byrd Flying Field) at Richmond. Byrd Field was the commercial airport serving Richmond and was also home for the Virginia Air National Guard's tactical fighter squadron that, at that time, was flying Republic F-105 aircraft. Col. Walter told me he would approve the use of a F-4E for a weekend cross-country flight to Richmond if I would get prior approval from the VANG squadron there. I called the Guard squadron at Byrd, and they were enthusiastic for a visit from a F-4. They said that it would be the first and that no other F-4 had ever flown into Richmond.

With Col. Walter's approval now secured, I got Howard Moss' quite happy support to go with me. He would get to see his parents, and the Institute.

On the appropriate day, I got into the front seat of a F-4E, and Howard Moss got into the back seat, and we launched for Richmond's Byrd Field.

Somewhere over North Carolina we descended below controlled airspace, cancelled our IFR clearance and proceeded VFR. Naturally, we detoured west to include a pass over Lexington.

With the Institute in sight, I let down so that I came over Alumni Hall at about 200 feet. I kept the speed down to about 450 knots so that we did not go by the Institute too quickly. As we passed Alumni Hall I continued letting down in altitude over the Parade Ground and then lit both afterburners. I would like to say that we flew between the flagpoles, but that is not possible; you cannot clear the barracks if you get that low. I will say that we were low and—being in afterburner—noisy, and now doing around 500-550 knots. As we passed over the barracks I pulled up into a vertical rolling climb.

The Institute was well and truly buzzed!

We proceeded on to Byrd Field at Richmond and landed there. We got absolutely wonderful treatment from the Air National Guard people there. We went to Howard Moss' parents' home, borrowed a car from them, and drove on to Lexington.

And that is how I got to my 20th class reunion, the first one for me, and how the Institute got buzzed.

22

Images

Houston H. (Tex) Carr, '59

Royall Geis running down the stoop at Step Off, breaking out light bulbs with a broom.

The sound of the drum, early one morning, as we experienced our first drumming out that foggy morning, my first morning at VMI.

Rats bracing in the mess hall.

First rat sentinel.

Hokie guard watching the visitors jump as we fired the evening gun.

Seeing girls on post on dance weekend. Once we gave them flowers.

The fright of Sunday Morning Inspection (SMI).

Sleeping in for SMI as I played a dance job (VMI Commanders) the night before; watching my roomies scurry around without me.

Forming up for classes.

Seeing the Texas flag on the Virginia flagpole on Texas Independence Day.

Watching the OD come thru the PX with his head bowed.

Getting my 10c coke and brownie at 10:00a.m. each morning of my Rat year and double-timing it up the stairs to my room for the feast.

Waiting in line to make a phone call to Sem.

The mailroom; the Dear John bulletin board on the first stoop.

Fireworks after taps.

Breaking out, in May. Getting our rings.

23

Jail Party

W.D. Meola, '52

In the fall of 1948 at VMI, as in all other colleges, we had a varsity football team and a freshman team. I played football at the prep school I had attended and I so indicated it on a questionnaire sent me by the Institute. I had unknowingly applied to play on the freshman (Rat) football team. On that team the Head Coach "Slick" Morton and Rat Coach C.T. Manley had recruited a number of prominent prep and high school players. One was Joe Fortunato who ended up playing linebacker for the Chicago Bears. When Slick moved on to Mississippi State several of the players he recruited went with him, Fortunato among them. I soon learned that my abilities were not good enough ever to get into a game much less get promoted to the varsity. I was assigned, along with several of my Brother Rats, to be "scrubs" for the varsity to practice against. We were instructed to do some of the things the scouts had seen the next week's opponent do, so the varsity would be prepared when they met on Saturday.

So what has this have to do with the story? Only this—even though I wasn't good enough to actually play football for VMI, I *was* eligible to sit on training tables. The Mess Hall had two types of tables, training tables and straining tables. At a straining table, Rats sat at attention, poured the milk, coffee, or iced tea, divided the dessert, entertained the upper classmen at the table with a new joke every night, and withstood whatever else upper classmen bedeviled you with. Often Rats would wait to eat until the upper classmen left the table. However, at the training table, you could relax. There were no upper classmen to bother you; therefore, eating at the training table was something very desirable.

When football season was over, I found out that the wrestling team would sit at a training table. Even though I had never formally wrestled, I went out for wrestling and made the team. At the end of the wrestling season, I looked around for another training table. There *was* to be one for the track team, but track season had not yet begun so, for a short time, I sat at a straining table. The upper classmen were only too happy to see me. For several months, I had managed to avoid a straining table, and now they saw their chance to initiate me to the "pleasures" of the straining table, Their pleasure, my pain. This lasted for about four weeks, until track season opened. I signed up for track, and once again got on training table.

Toward the end of the season, the Rat track team went to Blacksburg, Virginia for the state track meet. I had managed to make the track team as a javelin thrower. Varsity javelin throwers could pitch the javelin somewhere between 170 and 190 yards. The best I ever did was around 165 yards, and as hard as I tried, by altering my stride or the way I held the javelin, 165 yards was as far as I could throw it. After a freshman from VPI threw his javelin about 220 feet, I knew my track team days were over. This guy threw his javelin farther than our varsity could throw it. If he weighed 150 pounds, I'd be surprised, but when he let the javelin go, every fiber in his body went into the throw. The javelin quivered and made a beautiful arc in the air before it landed.

The javelin throw was one of the first events to be completed and afterwards we were allowed to roam the campus or go into the town of Blacksburg. I can't tell you who was with me; time has erased them from my memory, but there were about four of us. We were in uniform, so we didn't want to be conspicuous. It didn't matter; we went to town looking for some beer. In what we thought was a fairly deserted part of town, we went down a small street and around a corner and discovered a little beer parlor. After buying a six-pack of beer, we started to find a place to drink it. Being in uniform, sitting down on a curb was out of the question. We wandered around for a little while with the beer getting warmer all the time. Also, we didn't have a lot of time to waste, because we had to be back to our transportation for the trip back to the Institute, and we were getting a little panicky.

As we rounded the corner of a building, heading straight for us was a uniformed man. He had on a barracks type cap, and it had a metal emblem on it. All we needed was to be picked up by the Blacksburg police, and we could see penalty number one starring us in the face. He approached us and asked if we were looking for a place to drink our beer. He knew what we were doing and probably thought we were VPI cadets. With that, some of our anxiety was dispelled. He beckoned us to follow him. That we did until he took us around to the front of a building with a staircase up to an open second story door. He told us no one would bother us up there on the second floor but to close the door when we left. At the top of the stairs, we hesitated to go in the door, for what we were going into was the Blacksburg Jail. It had a number of cots lining both walls that we could sit on and was altogether a good place to drink beer. Although we were nearly satisfied our benefactor wasn't going to shut the door, we left it open and kept a jaundiced eye on it just in case. We found out later that the man was a fireman in uniform and was just trying to help out a bunch of boys trying to have a little fun. For a little while, however, we didn't know what our uniformed man had in mind and what our fate may have been.

I don't believe many others have ever had the opportunity to drink beer in the Blacksburg, Virginia jailhouse.

24

Jersey Rat Goes Executive

Erwin Hanke, '71

Like most rats who survived the initial culture shock of the first couple of months at VMI, I began to fall into a routine. Of the four of us, Andy Yurchak and I generally studied in the room, while Aaron Phillips and Steve Walker went out. One evening after SRC and CQ, I decided that I needed to do some reference work at the library, so I put my shirt back on, then donned my duty jacket and cap, and off I set at the required low trot down the ratline. Arriving at the reference room of Preston, my quick assessment of the area revealed that Mr. Province, Chairman of the Rat Disciplinary Committee, was there, accompanied by a young lady. For whatever reason, Mr. Province was not enjoying her company within the more secluded and comfortable atmospheres of LeJeune Hall or the Timmons record room. Oh, happy day. I decided to locate myself at a table distant from the couple, took off my jacket, and opened my notebook. Ah, what to do first? I needed to access a book right behind where Province was camped, so I quietly slid around the room, met his hard glance with a quiet "Good evening, Sir Ma'am," got my book and slithered back to my table. After a while, I became engrossed in my studies and forgot about my near death experience bearding the lion. I became so focused that I didn't notice a shadow over my shoulder until I heard whispered, "Where's your belt, Rat?" My hand flew to my waist. No belt! I checked the chair and the floor. No belt! In the process of re-dressing, I had forgotten to wrap that useless piece of webbing around my hips. Blood rushed to my face, and I turned to stone. "You are improperly dressed in public, Rat. In front of my girl, Rat. She is deeply offended, Rat. Drive by my room tomorrow after DRC." And he was gone.

Once my heart rate slowed back down to 160 beats per minute, I looked up. Province was back with his girlfriend, acting as if nothing extraordinary had happened. The rest of the people in the room also behaved normally. The earth continued to turn. The fluorescent lights continued to hum. But there had been a major shift in the alignment of the stars. I now had a personal invitation from the Chairman of the RDC for a private audience within his chambers for the express purpose of a little one-on-one, to be capped with the presentation of a 3x5 invitation to the Executive Committee.

Although he had not asked, and I had not volunteered, my name, I did not feel lucky enough at that point to test whether or not Mr. Province actually knew me from any other be-speckled, skinny, baldheaded Rat in the corps. Next day, I showed up at his room, directly from our march-up formation, still in blouse and straight pants. Either Province had gotten there just before me, or, more likely, he preferred the formality of wearing his blouse over class dyke for our little interview. He immediately ordered me into the front-leaning rest position, where I was better able to admire the handsome spit shine that he or his dyke had put on his low quarters. He leaned down to ask me Rat bible questions and unsatisfactory answers resulted in his inviting me to lower myself closer to the floor. As I did not quite meet his standards in either answering questions or in assuming the four-point horizontal "rest" position, I got to experience the abbreviated but effective Tom Province Upper Body Strength Development Program. As time was running out before both he and I had to report for class parade, he asked me one last question. As I had already set a new personal best performance for push-ups, I was well past my self perceived limit. To encourage me to reach new heights (paradoxically, with my nose near the floor), he placed his beautifully shined toe right under my chest, warning me not to touch it. No slow collapse for me. When I went down, I went down as hard as 136 pounds can go, right on that shiny toe. "Get up, Rat. There's your card. I'll see you at the next RDC meeting." Up I jumped, grabbed the card and my cap from the corner of the desk, and out I flew, careful to maintain a proper ratline trot as I squared my way back up to 417 to peel off my sweaty blouse and undershirt before changing for class. I went to the EC, "winning" my Triple Crown, but I never again went to the RDC (as a Rat). Of course, this wasn't my last trip to the EC. I reprised my Province EC appearance as a SE Third. But that's a story for another time.

25

Jersey Rat Meets the General Committee

Erwin Hanke, '71

I managed to take a Third Class privilege on the first day that the Old Corps returned to barracks after cadre. It seemed innocent enough, to venture out to an organizational meeting of the Civil War Roundtable after DRC. It was a misty evening, one of those nights when the late summer of Lexington couldn't quite decide whether or not to rain. Still intrigued with the variety of uniform items available to us, I decided to break out the rain cape. Before hitting the stoop, I turned back to my roommates to ask one last time if they would not join me in exploring our new school's part in history. Still too shell-shocked from cadre to leave the relatively secure confines of our room voluntarily, they all turned me down. I snapped up my cape, took my garrison cap in one hand, the door knob in the other, and out of Room 417 I charged, hoping to discover some of that youthful, martial spirit of our ante-bellum predecessors to sustain me through the next nine months.

Thirds could only visit the fourth stoop on official business, and such a one I immediately encountered. A Third on Official Business, that is. I quickly learned that he was not taking a class privilege in being up there, but I was. Taking a class privilege, that is. And the privilege taken was a Third Class privilege, i.e., "Improperly dressed on the stoop." Specifically, I had neglected to protect my cap with rain cap cover. Corporal Albright, sterling fellow that he was, recognized this as a "teachable moment" and he told me he was sending me up to the General Committee in recognition of my gross ignorance and negligence. So, instead of going to a meeting about history, I made a little "history" myself, as possibly the first GC'er of my class.

Of course, Mr. Albright didn't have a 3x5 card with him at the time of our encounter, so he said he would give it to me later. Well, he didn't give it to me at

BRC, or DRC or even SRC. For days, I experienced heart palpitations whenever I saw that corporal. I thought that maybe he was going to let me off, or had forgotten my little indiscretion. On the third day, he gifted me with my 3x5, the little bastion of righteousness. I actually made it up to the GC before the RDC. While not as common a "send up" as the RDC, making a General Committee function was not that rare an event. Ah, but the Executive Committee…That is a story for another time.

I survived the GC, despite the extra attention one garners at such an exclusive gathering. I almost felt like I was lost in the crowd when I later was worked over on my way up the steps to the RDC. I spent but a relatively few minutes before the Rat Disciplinary Committee itself, presided over by Mr. Tom Province. Mr. Province took his RDC chairmanship, like every aspect of his cadetship, very seriously. Hard, solid, he looked like he had been carved out of granite with blasting caps and a cold chisel. He carried himself with a practiced seriousness, and I don't recall him ever smiling or ever chastising a rat with anything but a measured whisper close to his penitent's ear. The average rat could feel Province's glinty, squinty, smoldering stare on the back of his head from a distance of ten yards, but by then, it was too late to escape. You could feel the stubs of what used to be hairs, now phantom fuzz, trying to stand up on the back of your neck. But too late. Nowhere to run to, baby. Nowhere to hide. Trapped. Like a rat.

A First would use Tom Province as the barracks boogieman. If his dyke wasn't getting him up early enough (or too early), wasn't getting his underwear folded correctly, or, God forbid, if he should get "boned" for "Dirt in waste can during SMI" due to a lack of adequate rattie diligence, the word wouldn't be, "If this happens again, I won't pick up your mail for you until after DRC," or "I won't let you go out Washington Arch with me to the next CP." If you weren't getting the sash pinned up straight by the second wrap, or if you screwed up the menu two days in a row, it was, "I'm going to send you down for a little visit to Tom Province's room." Yikes! Now *that* was a threat that generally had the desired effect. I must admit, in all fairness, that I didn't spend a lot of time around Province, so this may not be a fair assessment of his true demeanor. (Tom went on to W&L Law School; I'm not looking for a case of slander.) And, of course, my dyke never sent me to Province's room. He didn't have to. I sent myself. But that's another story.

26

Jersey Rat Meets the System

Erwin Hanke, '71

I don't claim that my class constitutes the last of the Old Corps, but I don't believe anyone would ascribe to us the title of "New Corps" either. I did not take notes during the incidents I am here reporting (had other things on my mind; posterity wasn't one of them, survival was), but the following account is substantially correct, so I don't expect to receive any fussy little notes correcting me on picayune details. Anyway, back in our version of the "Old Corps," in 19 and 67, my experience of matriculating to the VMI went something like this...

I don't remember Interstate 81, with its current, unofficial speed limit of Mach 2, being the approach used to get to Lexington. We used Route 11, passing through the string of quaint Valley towns that are usually by-passed today. As a consequence, New Jersey to Lexington was not a day trip, so the whole family trundled down in the family wagon (station, not horse-drawn) to deposit me into the waiting, loving arms of the Mother "I." As the Keydet-General and Robert E. Lee Hotels were booked, my family of five was crammed into the last room of the Barnes Motel in Buena Vista for the night. After a leisurely breakfast, we drove up to Limits Gate on Letcher Avenue to an angular corporal in white ducks, blouse, and white gloves (that were *not* rolled up to the first knuckle of his thumb), with his garrison cap pulled down so low we figured that he only knew of our car's approach by the sound of the wheels on the bricks.

Having stated that the purpose of our visit was to deposit the family's first-born as a sacrifice to the Virginia War Machine, we were instructed to drive around to Jackson Arch, where I was to unload and carry into the old courtyard all of my gear. (I hadn't realized what kind of hardship I was creating for myself by bringing a banjo and a typewriter.) I then followed the group of soon-to-be Brother Rats down to Cocke '94 Hall, where I was to be processed, while the rest of the family began their quest to find an available parking place among the three to five designated for such a purpose. I think they ended up in front of the Southern Inn on Main Street. The system worked as designed, and by the time they caught up with me and their breath, I and my squad were ready to officially enter barracks. The family was instructed to quickly take their leave of me, for I had a busy day scheduled. A hug, a kiss, a firm handshake, and I entered Jackson Arch for my second time, not casually as a "civvie" this time, but as an occupant of the ratline. Years later, my mother confided that she cried the whole trip back (she had wanted me to attend UVA), and that she fully expected me to reach home, by bus, before they did.

"Get in line. Move it! Immediately and forthwith! And I mean right NOW, maggot, you scum-sucking dung beetle!" I and my new Brothers had been suddenly transmigrated within the cosmic hierarchy from high school graduates, some real BMOCs, to just lower than whale sh*t in the North Atlantic. Weeks passed before our status improved. Once the football season began, we were informed that, as miserable examples of American youth that we were, we were to consider ourselves superior to Hokies, Minks, and Wahoo's. Of course, none of those guys were around except at games (check formations for us), and when we saw them, they seemed happy in their ignorance of their true station in life, distracted as they were by hair in their eyes, beers in their hands, and women in their lives. Poor fools. But I am getting ahead of myself.

Legend has it that Robert E. Lee passed through his entire cadetship at West Point without receiving a single demerit. Very impressive. I am not aware of what form of intra-corps discipline and behavior modification systems the USMA may have in place, but back in my day, the VMI corps had the RDC, the GC, and the EC. Not to belabor details before the cognoscenti, but the GC (General Committee) was/is the system responsible for ensuring that class privileges were not abused. Class privileges consist, primarily, of each class having the "right" to breach Institute regulations. Then there were "privileges" officially extended to even rats, but not by the GC (such as crossing the parade ground [3rd Class] or walking in the mess hall [1st Class]). Of course, if caught in any GC-sanctioned infringement by the Administration, you were on your own, but clever cadets could run their own risk/gain analyses. Being reported for breaking a class privilege could earn a cadet penalty tours and/or confinement, but not the dreaded demerits that Lee successfully negotiated. The RDC (Rat Disciplinary Committee) was/is an organization administered by the First Class to enforce all of the special conventions required of New Cadets, beyond those imposed upon the rest of the student body by the Administration or the GC. The EC (Executive Committee) was composed of the student leaders charged with the awesome task of keeping the VMI corps' reputation in the Real World untarnished, i.e., responsible for dealing with any member of the corps that misbehaved in public like he was a real college student.

During the course of the ratline, most of us managed to get caught in an information-deficit mode at some point, for not knowing the Inscription on the Parapet, or how many links are in the chain surrounding Washington's statue, or the menu for the next meal. Or we didn't deport ourselves with the proper military bearing while hoofing it down the ratline, or couldn't hold a pencil between our shoulder blades long enough. Any of these failings or a myriad of others could earn one a 3x5 card, an invitation in the not-too-distant future to attend an after hours "party" with a few dozen of your close, personal Brother Rats, hosted by a few of the First Class elite, then held in the "penthouse" over Jackson Arch. Returning to one's room after DRC or evening study to find your formal "invitation" to the soirée of the evening had a chilling effect on not only the recipient, but also on the roommates, especially early in our cadetships, when the creepy-crawly, cold-sweat-running-down-your-spine feeling was still new. Many loving, caring First Class dykes considered the RDC encounter to be so fundamental to the whole VMI experience that they would send up their own rats to the RDC if the trip had been somehow dodged. I did not force my dyke, Frank Pinizzotto, into having to make such a "tough love" decision. While I didn't set any RDC attendance records, I did make the trip more than once. Not a big deal; most, if not all, of my Brother Rats made the RDC. A greater distinction was being sent up to the GC. But that is a story for another time.

27

Jiggs and Big N

Houston H. (Tex) Carr, '59

I was one of the EE's in the class of '59. There always seemed to be twenty-three of us, from our Rat year on. The head of the EE Department (the computer had not been invented yet so there was no computer science) was Col. Jamison, affectionately referred to as Jiggs behind his back. (Not sure if his wife was Maggie.) The other senior EE instructor was Lt. Col. Lee Nichols, Asst. Commandant, referred to as 'N'. We lived in fear of both these men.

The following shows the two sides of Jiggs. One afternoon, in class in the basement of Nichols Hall, a low ceiling basement classroom with no windows, Jiggs was conducting a course in electrical production and distribution. One of the class went to sleep (remember the room is dark and it's afternoon). Instead of hollering or shaking the man, Jiggs picked up a piece of lead sheath cable and slammed it down on the desk with a sound that would have raised the dead. The sleeping student did, indeed, come to consciousness. For some reason, we all seemed a bit more attentive after that.

On another day, Jiggs's wife picked him up in front of the Hall. They seemed to be at odds, and he was not quick enough in getting into the vehicle, so she started driving away, with Jiggs running to get into the car. Jiggs was not in particularly good shape, so running is relative. He did get into the car.

As for Big N, he could be human but seldom let it show. In one class, when we were second semester Firsts, I had my Dad, who owned a printing plant, create for us TS Cards. These are cards that will be punched when something pitiful happens to the holder. I gave the cards to N to pass out in our class; the signature of the card was 'Just E Nuf' (a favorite saying of Jiggs) and it was signed N. Col. Nichols told us that the final exam in his class qualified everyone for a free punch. He was correct, especially for me as of the two ways to solve the major problem, I took the long way around. After our final exam, which stood in our way to graduation, when we were all waiting for grades, N came out and chatted with us for a long time. Only then did we believe he had good wishes for us.

28

Just Let Me Sleep

Nathaniel Southworth, (Aric), '94

As a rat, my roommates were Fred Barber and Doug Estes. We were the oddest of roommates. Fred was an athletic wrestler/football player from Columbus, Georgia, who spoke with a mild and almost feminine Southern accent. Doug was a pampered Southern boy from the Eastern Shore of Virginia, and I was a cocky beanpole who spent too much time playing practical jokes. One morning, at six a.m., we had a morning company room inspection. While Fred and I had set the alarm clock for 0430 in order to have ample time to prepare, Doug came in from studying after taps while we were asleep and reset the alarm for 0530 because he had already taken care of *his part of the inspection.* (BRF meant something to Fred and I at this point!) Needless to say when the alarm went off, Fred and I barely had enough time to get out of our racks before the Cadre burst into our room, screaming. Well, room 469 had just earned all our marvelously happy brother rats in Delta Company a 0500 inspection the next day!

As you can imagine, our BR's were not pleased. We needed to shine on the next inspection. Room 469 was ready to redeem itself, so in outstanding fashion, Fred, Doug, and I agreed to set our alarm for 0300 in order to have two full hours to prepare. The next morning when the alarm went off at 0300, we all sat up bleary-eyed, I turned off the alarm, and one by one we all thought we'd just put our heads on our pillows for a second or two, wipe the sleep out of our eyes and get ready for the task at hand. Boy, those racks sure were warm and comfortable when you're a cadet, even more warm and comfortable when you're a rat. You see what's coming don't you. The next sound I heard was a boot on our door, followed by a lot of screaming, followed by Fred, Doug, and myself being overturned in our beds and lying sprawled out on the floor. After the D Company Cadre left our room, or the ruins of what used to be our room, a purple cloud of screams, hollers, and yes, a bit of profanity lingered for a few moments while Doug, Fred and I all looked at each other dumbfounded and speechless. In case you were wondering, room 469 had just earned all our marvelously happy brother-rats in Delta Company a 0400 inspection the next day!

An image that will always be with me: after our entire company of angry D Company BR's piled into our room, Fred Barber was wringing his hands, saying in his soft Southern voice, "I know, I know, I'm so sorry. Feel free to throw some of our stuff around!"

29

Just Trust Me

Bill Bradley, '75

Excitement was in the air in the fall of 1974. The VMI/VPI football game was scheduled in Richmond, and my roommates talked of a prank to needle our rivals at Virginia Tech. My roommate Mike Farris mentioned that he was high school buddies with Tech's Regimental commander. The seed was planted, and we asked Mike to call the Regimental Commander and set up a supper to discuss a bet on the football game. The real plan was to kidnap him and hold him hostage until the game was over. The arrangements were made and a place was picked for our dinner.

Wednesday afternoon, Mike Mueller, Lowrie Tucker, Salvo, and I traveled to Blacksburg for our meeting. Mike Mueller was our enforcer, a Marine that carried the nickname *Ironman*. Our first stop was near the Tech barracks where we asked the first person we saw, a bandsman, for directions to his R/C. We identified ourselves as VMI keydets, and he looked at us with a high degree of suspicion and unmitigated dislike, but he led us straight to our target. Doug was relaxing in his room, and we were struck by how similar our rooms in barracks were to his. We engaged in some innocuous chatter about the game and told Doug we needed to go to supper as our time was limited. His roommates playfully reminded us not to kidnap their R/C. Our seating arrangements were prearranged with Salvo driving and Lowrie also in the front with Doug wedged between Mike and myself.

Doug realized that he was in trouble as we sped by our projected restaurant. Gleefully, we informed him that he was being kidnapped but as a salve to our conscience we asked if he would miss any important tests this week. He said no and accepted being our hostage with an open mind. We saw his integrity and realized why he was Tech's R/C. Dutifully, we fed him supper at a truck stop in Lexington and then returned promptly to barracks.

Within minutes, the news spread like wildfire, and the whole VMI corps knew of our kidnapping. Our own R/C dutifully informed our commandant, Buck Buchanan, of the sketchy details. For reasons that still escape me, the guilty parties were never called before the Commandant for an explanation. Doug, for the next couple of days, became a member of the Corps, attended classes, ate at the mess hall, and slept in barracks. He used the kidnapping as a learning experience and our admiration only grew for him. He traveled with us in buses as the Corps was transported to Richmond for the Saturday game. We lost the game but we had scored a small moral victory and learned an important lesson in grace under pressure. One last note, I would have liked to have seen that bandsman's expression when told his regimental commander had been kidnapped.

30

The Kangaroo Mascot of 1955

Houston H. (Tex) Carr, '59

The year before the Stonewall Class matriculated, the mascot kangaroo died. We needed a mascot, so we borrowed a young kangaroo from a local private zoo. I believe we named it Big Red. The animal was brought out to the pep rallies and football games by two cadet handlers. As time went on, the mascot became more difficult to handle, even with a strong guy on each of two ropes. We soon learned that the mascot was a female and that she was pregnant. Gee, wonder why she was difficult to handle?

31

Keydet Wiley Coyote

Houston H. (Tex) Carr, '59

The Corps had one weakness! It's sad, but true. One of the theaters in town, knowing of this weakness, would show six, back-to-back, full color *Roadrunner* and *Wiley Coyote* cartoons on a Wednesday afternoon. When the Corps returned from afternoon classes, or LA Beach, as was the case for some, many in the Corps would hurry to the theater to be sure to get inside. The place was full and not at all quiet. After a wonderful time in the visual arts, some of the Keydets would continue their culture endeavors in the back room of the College Inn. (Yes, I have been in this establishment, as the Commanders played several dance jobs for the Minks.) A wonderful afternoon was had by all, except for those touring the countryside, complements of the Commandant's Office.

32

Late Dating a Mink

Koontz, Warren, '53

During the summer between our third and second class years, I had a job as a room clerk at the Mountain Lake resort in southwest Virginia. The hotel employees had an opportunity to use the facilities at the resort when not in use by hotel guests. A horse and I had a disagreement and I ended up with a broken femur (thighbone). On returning to VMI that fall, I was in a hip spica cast from chest down to the toes of my right leg. I could go to class on crutches but lived for the first two months in the infirmary. During a dance weekend at Washington and Lee, I received a phone call from a young lady who was attending the dances at W&L. She agreed to pick me up at the infirmary around 1:00 a.m. for a late date. Since the minks had late dates with girls VMI cadets invited to its dances, I thought it was appropriate to turn the tables. I knew there was no stick check at the infirmary and so the young lady (name withheld to protect the innocent) picked me up and returned me to the alley just north of the infirmary around 4:30 a.m.

33

Lexington Express, Anyone?

Bill Noell, '53

During our First Class year, BR Bill Nelson and I succeeded in causing the Lexington train, chugging up the tracks behind barracks one afternoon, to start slipping and sliding, and momentarily stop during our Chemistry Lab as it made its way up the 'grade' to the Lexington station on the other side of Washington and Lee.

Now, this was not an original idea of mine as it was generated by one of the Old Corps stories passed down by my father, Class of '24. But in his time, the Lexington train was loaded with gals coming in for one of the VMI Hops, the way my mother used to travel from Sullins College in Bristol. However, the greasing of the tracks by Bill and me brought on the same effect as it did when my father did it twenty eight years earlier, only we did not bring on the crowd to witness the struggling train loaded with freight, as the previous feat did when it was loaded with Hop Dates yelling out the windows towards barracks.

Now with all the passing of time of fifty years, I am not sure how I got Bill Nelson interested in partaking of this venture, but evidently he liked the idea. Nor do I remember why and what date we picked, except it had to happen during our Chemistry Lab, Organic. So, one evening just after SRC had been completed, Bill and I stayed in the mess hall until all the Corps had departed. We then proceeded to gather a large quantity of the left over butter from the tables into two containers. In those days the butter was not recycled, but the excess was carried off by the mess hall crew. After we had two large containers filled, we went back to our rooms, to study (?) and to wait for the late hours of the night.

Sometime after Taps and barracks now being quiet, Bill and I made our way out of barracks, and down behind the old Chemistry Building, Maury Brook Hall, before the Annex. It was not exactly a good night as I recall, kind of cool and messy, as we climbed down the steep slope behind the chemistry building to the "Nile" and up and across. Now, in those Old Corp days, there was nothing on the other side of the Nile but woods, the clearing for the track, and a small dirt road way up behind the Supt's house going over to the "Cliffs." As we made our way down the hill, trying to hang on to the containers of butter with one hand, and holding on to trees/branches, etc. to keep from falling, and wondering if we would get caught and/or make it back before "stick check" as planned, we found that this getting to the tracks in the pitch dark was not as quick and easy as we had assumed.

After finally arriving at the tracks, we picked a lower section of tracks, and started greasing both rails for about fifty feet or more. We then skipped about fifty feet, moving up the tracks, then greased about another fifty feet. Now the section of track picked was well in view from the Chemistry Lab back windows, up on the third floor. After the task was completed, we made our way back to barracks. To our great satisfaction, especially since it had taken much longer than anticipated, we had completed the task prior to the stick check and thus were safe and sound, although tired, scratched up somewhat, muddy, and cold.

Then came the anticipation and keeping quiet until that afternoon lab. As usual, the lab started off in its normal, not too exciting routine, until one BR in the lab yelled that the train was out back again, but it was having some kind of problem on the tracks, so most rushed to the windows to see what was up, and I understand that some of the Corps on the backside of barracks witnessed the problem.

Anyway, the train contacted the first section of greased tracks, and part way up, the drive wheels started slipping on the tracks, and the train lost headway. After pouring on more steam, the train made it through that first section, and then suddenly hit the second section as the 'grade' increased. It bogged down to a momentary stop, until it "cranked up" the steam, and the spinning drive wheels wore down the butter on the tracks. Slowly, it moved forward and finally made it on to the clean track and went onto level track on its way into Lexington. However, for some reason, I cannot actually recall whether at one point, if the train slipped backwards somewhat, as it did when the "Hop Dates" experienced the event. Nevertheless, I am certain that the Engineer on that train was not too happy with the antics of two members of the VMI Corps on that day. We never heard anything about the event, however, after that day. It certainly did not make the local or VMI paper, or the "Turnout," but it did brighten up one Organic Chemistry Lab afternoon back there in 1952-1953. The next time home, when I recounted the tale to my father, he just smiled, but my mother had a few choice words on the event, such as that this was not the subject matter for which I went to the Institute. But my roommate and fellow Chemistry major, Pete Cox, thought it was great. Somehow, I had kept it from him until it occurred, and said it sounded like something his father, '20, would have done. But no longer is there a train, or tracks, behind barracks to challenge anyone in the Corps these days.

And yes, Bill Nelson and I both passed our Chemistry courses and went on to graduation as members of the Class of '53. Q.E.D.

34

Life with Moe

David Schwab, '73

During my Rat year, the Corps collected money to purchase a mascot. By the next year sufficient funds had been raised, a suitable animal had been found, purchased, and named "Moe."

Moe was a wallaby, a miniature kangaroo if you will, and a female (the first female to "attend" VMI?) The Institute found a "home" for her behind the biology building.

In May of 1971, I signed on as one of Moe's keepers, and I became the head keeper during my First Class year.

Caring for Moe wasn't particularly unusual, but there were some things about her that the general public didn't know, and one of those would get me in a bit of hot water with the Corps. Here are some interesting tidbits about Moe:

Moe was about the size of a big cat. She looked like a big rat that had a long tail and stood on its rear legs. The tail was mostly muscle; the rest of her was pretty delicate. She had big eyes and flashy eyelashes (yes, eyelashes).

As cute as she was, Moe had a nasty personality. She hissed a lot and wasn't exactly the huggable type. Fortunately for the keepers, she didn't bite, but the way she glared at us said, "Leave me alone!"

Moe's diet was mostly vegetables, especially cucumbers. She loved cucumbers. One of us would stop in at the mess hall kitchen each day to collect her rations. When necessary, I managed to get "Red" Turner to donate something from the kitchen at the PX.

Moe had a roommate: a rabbit. I have no idea where it came from and don't know what happened to it. The bunny was there just to keep Moe company.

People ask if Moe had a pouch. Of course she did—she was a marsupial; it was about the size of a half dollar.

We often exercised Moe on the parade field, usually during military duty, but only when it was clear. Moe had a tendency to want to run and hide, and it would be real easy for someone to step on her. She hopped about just as you might expect, and it was necessary for at least two of us to run along with her. Once she had gone far enough, one of us would collect her by grabbing her tail and swinging her into our arms.

Moe's tail was all muscle and the toughest part of her body. If we tried to pick her up any other way while on the run, we risked injuring her. For the same reason, we didn't want to put a leash on her.

Of course, we brought Moe to all the home games. She drew a lot of attention at ball games, especially from kids and pretty girls. Being a keeper wasn't a bad job.

During halftime at one football game, we made arrangements to run with her down the center of the field. We ran with her just as we exercised her, and the Corps cheered. When I felt we had gone far enough, I grabbed her by the tail, and the Corps booed. What a kick in the pants that was. I had to make the trek up to the observation booth to get someone to make an announcement why we picked Moe up the way we did. In those days the Corps wasn't beyond wetting down even a First Classman's room if he displeased them.

35

Light the Tree

Alan Toler, '83

Every year before exams, the corps would form up on the stoops for SRC Christmas Dinner. I don't remember all the particulars during formation—whether there was music by the band or songs by the choral group or both or even any. I do remember the uniform was overcoat; the temperature was always cold, and the stoops got dark when the lights were turned out. The last command before the corps marched to SRC was 'Light the Tree'.

The tree stood on top of the sentinel box and would be lit in the evening, very uplifting for everybody. I will never forget rat year, comforter over the transom, studying late in my room for the last exam…this reminds me of a story:

'Twas the night before last exam when all through the corps not a rat was stirring not even the TAC *officer*. The Christmas tree was decorated by the stoopies with care, in hopes that the break would soon be here. The remaining Keydets were nestled all snug in their racks, while visions of As, Bs, Cs, and Ds danced in their heads. I had just awoke from an exam power nap, when, out on the courtyard, there rose such a clatter, 'Light the Tree' was the matter. Away to the stoop I flew like a flash, tore open the door and did the fifty yard dash. The FIRE on the tree melted the new fallen snow and gave a luster of mid-day to the eyes below, when, what to my wondering eyes should appear but a rat sentinel with fire fighting gear. I knew at that moment that Christmas was near, and somebody else would try it next year. And 'you know the rest of the story'.

This was an annual tradition for the academicians who spread out their exams. I remember my first class year it was the night before the last exam, and I knew somebody would keep the tradition. I believe it took one bed sheet torn in strips, half gallon of Girl Scout water, and a light source fixed to the end of a pole. You sure missed a pretty sight if your exams were over early.

36

Matriculation Day

Lance Pickering, '88

Matriculation Day is a very traumatic experience for every VMI alumnus. It is not always remembered very vividly, because the day is so traumatic that it becomes a blur of sights and sounds in memory. I'm sure many alumni would just prefer to forget this day and try to blot it from their mind. Nevertheless, I do have a couple of specific memories that come to mind when I think back to my matriculation.

As football players, my teammates and I were scheduled to go through the matriculation line first. This was so we could go through the essential portions of matriculation before practice. Of course, we all thought we had a leg up on the rest of our BR's, because we had already been on Post for a week with the football team. This meant that we'd heard all about what to expect from our upperclass teammates. Of course, as anybody from VMI can tell you, nothing can actually prepare you for the actual experience. Anyway, I got the bright idea that it would be really cool to be first in line, and the first one to sign The Book. (Note: The Book is a book containing the signatures of everybody who has ever matriculated at VMI.) Boy, was I wrong! I soon found out what a dumb idea that was! What it ended up meaning was that I was the first rat exposed to the Cadre, and I got just a little extra time in their "loving" hands. As I walked down the tunnel in Cameron Hall, as the proverbial lamb to the slaughter, I could see a slight smile creasing the lips of the waiting Cadre. I also could have sworn that there was a slight bit of drool at the corners of their mouths as they awaited their first victim—me.

One thing we had constantly been told in the week leading up to matriculation was, "Don't lose your Rat Bible." (Note: The Rat Bible is a little book every rat carries containing all of the information about VMI a rat is supposed to know. A rat is supposed to memorize every word in it.) Over and over, we heard, "Whatever you do, don't lose your Rat Bible."

Of course, I was determined that I would not commit this grievous sin. On matriculation day, after we had received our Rat Bibles along with a lecture as to its importance, we were led to our rooms to change into "idiot dyke." (This was the rat uniform consisting of white shirt, utility trousers, low quarters, and utility cover.) Upon entering my room, I put my Rat Bible on my desk and started to change. I no sooner had done this than a sergeant walked in, scooped up my Rat Bible, and walked out. I couldn't believe it! I hadn't had my Rat Bible five minutes, and I'd already lost it! The one thing we were warned not to let happen, and I'd already done it! I was crestfallen! I was also thinking that this was not a very good start to my cadetship and did not bode well for my future. Luckily, the sergeant brought it right back along with a few choice words about taking care of my Rat Bible. I did learn my lesson though. I never lost my Rat Bible again. In fact, I still have it today.

One final note on matriculation day: it was the only time in my life when I was actually looking forward to football practice.

37

Mickey Mouse

Houston H. (Tex) Carr, '59

It seems that the recent situations with the Minks tend to concentrate on Red Square. We marched to church by several of the frat houses and the brothers were often on the balcony, with dates, with hangovers. In their conditions, with even duller brains, they would sometimes taunt the church details, sometimes with the Mickey Mouse song. On one occasion, while I was there, a BR heading the Episcopal detail stopped the detail in front of a frat house, called for left face, and pointed an outstretched hand at the balcony. The music stopped and stayed stopped. The next Sunday, their senior class president and our First Class president were on Red Square to monitor the action. All was quiet on the western front.

I understand that, on another occasion, the church detail did the honor of going into the offending frat building and cleaning house. We are, after all, nice guys at heart—irritable on Sunday, but nice!

38

Muscle Power

Art Pomponio, '59

Back in our third class year of 1957, I had the misfortune to have Colonel Byrne as my calculus instructor. As some of you may remember, Colonel Byrne was head of the Math Department and an outright math genius. He would face the class and as he explained a calculus concept, he would write an example problem behind his back on the blackboard. I guess I was so overwhelmed by that feat that I never understood what he was teaching, and I failed the class. Our choices were to make up failed classes in summer school or retake the class the next year. I chose summer school and reported to VMI in mid July 1957.

I roomed with Jim "Big Jim" Wood and Bill "Fats" Lee. Colonel Axe taught the calculus class on a humans level and we all, including Jim, Sam Gillespie and Bobby Dale, were getting great grades with minimum study. Jim Wood and Bill Lee had a harder time with their classes in the EE Department with Colonel Nichols. We had plenty of free time, so Bill, Jim and I would jump into my Plymouth and go girl hunting. We began to get desperate until one day Jim came into the room and announced that he had gotten us blind dates with "town girls." I believe to this day that Jim got one of the stoop workers to set us up. But Jim said the girls were so great that their parents sent them away during the school year to keep them away from VMI and W&L guys.

Well, we met the girls, and I then knew that they were away during the school year, because they had jobs in the sideshow of a traveling circus. We went to Goshen for a night picnic and, after a few beers and a couple of hotdogs, we each went our separate ways with beer, blanket, and girl in that order of priority. Halfway through a heated discussion with my date on nuclear fission, I heard Jim shouting, "Let go, GD it, let go." Needless to say, I raced over to Jim to see what exactly Jim wanted his date to "let go" of. To my surprise, she was lying on the blanket, Jim was standing, and his date was holding his ankle with one hand. Jim could not kick free. We all remember that Jim wrestled heavyweight and 177 lb on the VMI team with Skip White, "Little" Jim Wood, and Don Basham, so he was no little guy. But this girl was so big and strong that Jim had to promise her something before she would let him go. He would never tell Bill or me what he promised. I do know that it ruined the evening, and it was the last time Jim ever was in charge of dates, and it was the last time any of the three of us ever dated a "town girl."

I promised Jim that summer of 1957 that I would never tell any of his brother rats that his date was bigger and stronger then him, but I now consider this revelation covered under *The Freedom of Information Act.*

Thanks, Jim, for the memory.

39

New Cadet Shoes

David Schwab, '73

Like most Rats, I struggled hard to learn the art of spit shining shoes and cartridge boxes. One day, a First Classman provided me with the solution to all my shine problems: spit shine in a can! For a small fee I could have an instant shine on my leather goods. Wasn't life great?!

I couldn't believe my good fortune. As quick as I could, I shined my shoes.

That evening I got ready for SRC, confident that the upperclassmen in Alfa Company would be amazed that this Rat had done such a stellar job on his shoes. I assumed the position as I stepped out of room 454 and followed the Ratline out Jackson Arch to my assigned place in the Alfa Company ranks. It didn't take long for a Second Classman to approach. I popped to…he was looking at my shoes.

"I'll bet you sprayed your shoes with that shine in a can, didn't you, Rat?"

"How did he know that?" I thought. I said, "Yes, sir," but the puzzled look on my face must have betrayed me.

"Look at your shoes, Rat." I looked down. White streaks covered my shoes. I was horrified.

The brilliant finish on my shoes was destroyed wherever the shoe was flexed.

I took solace in the fact that I was not the only Rat who had fallen victim to the can of instant shoeshine.

40

Nine Years Later

Edmund R. Strickler, '62

I graduated from VMI in 1962 and my brother, Michael, graduated in 1971. Being a good brother, I attended his graduation. Just prior to the graduation parade, I had drunk more than my allotted share of bourbon and decided to head for the barracks and see Michael before his final parade. I was talking with Michael and his roommates, and they jokingly said, "Why don't you march in the Parade?" Wrong thing to say. I told them that if they found a uniform I would. (At that time I could still get into one.) Several minutes later I was "dyked out" and ready to go even though my hair would not have passed inspection. They placed me in the back of a company in the far reaches of the courtyard hoping I wouldn't be discovered. I wasn't, and when we marched out of Jackson Arch, I was on my way. As we marched onto the Hill, a rat behind me said that the next movement would be a "column right". I said, "Quiet, Rat! I've been in one hell of a lot more of these than you." That was the last I heard from him.

The parade went off without incident, and I got back to barracks and distributed "my uniform" back to its proper owners. It was great fun.

The interesting thing about doing this was that, even with the extra bourbon, everything came back to me. The rifle manual, the various commands, and the beat of the drum were as if I had never left. I guess, in many ways, I never have, and I know I never will.

41

Officer in Charge

Houston H. (Tex) Carr, '59

Each guard team had two cadet officers and an Institute officer, the Officer-in-Charge (OC). The OC would show up occasionally in addition to making his nightly stick check and would sleep in barracks, in the OC's Hole, which was a room/office off of Washington Arch. Some OC's were liked by the Corps more than others. One, for example, was a real pain and was really on a tare one day. This was not well received by the Corps. He walked through Washington Arch once too often and was welcomed with a bucket of water. By the time he could see again from the water, there was no one on the stoop above him. Not sure of his ultimate actions, but I think he got the word.

On another occasion, the OC has done something worthy of retaliation. Several cadets gathered enough old newspaper to completely fill the OC's Hole with wadded up newspaper, and I do mean completely. As I remember, you could barely get the door open to take the paper out.

42

Out of the Frying Pan

Erwin Hanke, '71

Like so many VeeMees back in the 60's, I began my career in higher education as engineer, civil, one (1) each. The Engineering Department was probably the biggest at VMI, with a reputation throughout the Commonwealth as large as a VMI class ring. I had taken tests several years before that had convinced my family that I was a natural engineer, so, naturally, engineering was my first choice of majors. Somewhere deep into that midnight sun period of my second semester, while taking a five-hour math course, it occurred to me that I was *not* a natural mathematician. My proficiency with a slide rule was such that if I had not been able to scratch my back with it, it would have been of no use to me at all. I had taken all required math in high school; we had been on speaking terms, Algebra I, Algebra II, and Calc. Not friends, but we would nod in the hall. You know, that sort of thing. But this Five-Hour Math. I tried to be nice. I spent time trying to get to know it. I kept the book close to me, but I kept falling asleep when it was trying to tell me something it thought was really important. It just wasn't working out. So it dumped me. Flat. First my girl, then my Math. What a winter. But I wouldn't, couldn't accept it. Math was too important for me to just let go. My advisor told me that I really needed to give it another try.

The summer after rat year, I took an equivalent five-hour Math at Rutgers. We spent that summer together, and this time, Math and I seemed to get along better, but it was just an empty "C" relationship. By the time I was to return to Lexington, I had grown resentful, and couldn't see myself spending the rest of my life with Math. I had to get out of the relationship while I still had my dignity. Of course, giving up Math also meant giving up Engineering. So much for that life's dream. But give it up for what?

It didn't take a rocket scientist to figure out that I couldn't become a rocket scientist, or any kind of scientist, without Math. Serious Math. Lotsa Math. Could have gone to English or History, but I had my pride. (I had spent too much time making fun of my LA brethren.) My German professor tried to convince me to switch to German as my major. Still, any of these would have been fine if I wanted to teach, but what kind of contradictory statement would I be making by going to *THE* premier military college to become a teacher? It was not like I was a State Cadet. No way. Wasn't going to happen. So what were my options? Slim and none. I chose Slim.

Economics. Not Business Administration, or Management, or Communications or any of those subtle but different majors that "students" attending "college" could take and master. Economics. The mysterious, quasi-science perpetrated against those innocent seekers of a practical, non-science course of study at the Institute. Fraternities and secret societies had been banned from VMI back when F.H. Smith was running things, but there in the dungeon of Scott Shipp Hall, Colonel Morrison presided over the new degree-awarding Department of the Esoteric and Arcane, a cult surely as impenetrable and Machiavellian as the Molly McGuire's. Economics. I thought that this course represented my most promising future. Anyone who could translate Economics into English would have the Keys to Success. What I did not know at the time was that Col Morrison was experiencing challenges of his own.

The Colonel was determined that his program would be among the best. His plan must have been to grow the department slowly, with 28 members of the Class of 1968 so enrolled, 29 in '69, and 21 in '70, but 46 were listed among the Class of 1971. This last statistical outlier must have concerned the Colonel, threatening his plan and taxing his faculty. So, if the program was to reach its goal, success was not to be found in numbers. If VMI was not a boat in a sea of grade inflation, then Economics was not even a kiddie float. If you could not swim, and swim well, you were going to drown. Many cadets found themselves unequal to the challenge. The days following the posting of grades saw many would-be economists darkening Col Morrison's office door with requests to transfer to History or English or Anything else. This was the situation in the "Root Cellar" as I found myself before the Colonel.

After the exchange of salutes and as I laid my transfer form on the desk before him, Col Morrison asked why I was there. "Cadet Hanke reporting to discuss the changing of majors, sir," I stated. With a long, tired face, the colonel looked down, expressionless. "Have you given this decision a lot of thought?" he asked. "Yes, sir," I replied. "Have you discussed this with your faculty advisor?" "Yes, sir, I have. I am having too much difficulty with the math." He continued with, "Have you talked about this change and its effect on your future with your parents? This is a big decision, not to be taken lightly, nor in haste." I assured him that all concerned had given the question due consideration.

Resigned to the change, Colonel Morrison began to look down to sign the transfer form which would bring me into the fold as an Econ student. He gave a long, low sigh and raised his pen as he asked, "Into what major do you want to transfer?" When informed that my request was to transfer *into* Economics, he felt honor-bound to warn me that I had a "long row to hoe." His warning went unheeded.

By the graduation of the Class of 1971, the original forty-six and I had dwindled to fifteen brothers. It wasn't pretty and it wasn't easy, but I was one of those few. And I still have the calluses and scars to prove it.

43

Penny Annoyance

Alan Toler, '83

I had forgotten this story until one of my next door BR's (Nate, Jim, Tim, Mark) reminded me at our ten-year reunion. It was the fall of our third class year. My next door BR's were having a little problem with the occupants above. You can remember how loud things sounded in the room below. The rats would drop pennies on the floor almost all evening which had been going on long enough, a couple of weeks. No matter how much my BR's strained the rats, they did not slow up. It would seem their dykes were constantly getting them out of the ratline. By coincidence, their dykes lived directly below on the first stoop. You might say that it was only pennies, but believe me that constant noise gets under your skin pretty fast.

Since I was playing rugby at the time, something had to be done. Of course, we knew better than to tell the plan. One evening practice was over about the time the corps marched to SRC. Once in the perpetrator room, the sink was stuffed, the water turned on as hard as it would go, all racks flipped over, and the door sealed. I proceeded to shower and form up for SRC with the rugby club. Unfortunately, even after the rats left the mess hall they would be drilled by the cadre till the 19:30 stick check. I was not present to see the water activities, but my next door BR said it looked 'like a big 'ole waterfall coming off the fourth stoop'. I did not realize the rooms were not water tight till the first stoop. You guessed it, some water went right down the walls and started to fill it up. Boy, were there some upset firstclassmen.

After I returned from SRC, I heard the firstclassmen locking my BR's heels trying to find out who did this. No matter how much they yelled and screamed, nobody got in trouble. How much damage can a lot of water do? Needless to say problem solved.

Class of '83—1/Rats—0

44

Prophesy

Bruce Mackenzie '59

I remember the second day when we were all lined up by height on the parade ground. After the Cadre was satisfied that we were in proper order, a command was given. We were told to stand at ease and to look at the person's name in front of us and behind us, because neither would be present at graduation! I made a mental note. When I returned to my room, #419, I wrote down those two names on a post card. I sent this card with some type of note to my dad. By the way, I was in "D" Company.

When I graduated, my dad brought that post card to me. Neither name on the card was present. I don't know what happened to that card, but the impression of that statement has never left me.

45

Rain?

Eddie Fall, '59

In my room were four different young men: Bob Ross, the well-known football coach; Ray Conklin, who went to VMI for six years and still no degree; Donnie Dreelin, a real jock man, who was always laughing and cutting up, and myself, Eddie Fall, better known as "Baldy."

One Saturday, Donnie, and I went uptown. We drank about ten beers apiece and proceeded to walk back to the Institute. Arriving just before taps, we hurried to bed and fell fast asleep. Baldy woke up needing to relieve himself. The room was freezing with both windows open. Donnie Dreelin stood at the windows. Bobby Ross told Donnie and myself that I had relieved myself out of the window, returned to my rack, and went back to sleep. The problem was that the flow of water was falling on Dreelin's bed!

The next morning, Dreelin asked if it had rained. We asked him why, and he said he had found a frozen puddle at his feet. Bobby Ross laughed so hard he almost fell over.

46

Rat Bites

Pickering, Lance, '88

As a "football rat," I, along with my teammates, had the luxury of eating our meals at the training table, where we did not have to sit at attention or strain during the meal. We simply ate in peace. One of our team captains was also a ranker and, during Cadre week, he got the "wonderful" idea that we should eat a meal with the Cadre like the rest of our BR's in order to learn what it was like. So, it was decided that at DRC (lunch to the uninitiated), we would eat with the Cadre. All we knew going in was that you sat at attention on the front three inches of your chair and that you couldn't look down. Also, we were told that you stopped eating and strained if an upperclassman addressed you. I don't think this adequately prepared us for the upcoming meal.

On this particular day, the meal was foot-long hot dogs. Once the meal was served, we started eating, doing our best to remain inconspicuous so as not to incur the wrath of the Cadre. Unfortunately, this was not to be. At least not for Tim White who was sitting across from me. Tim used to get a lot of attention from the Cadre mainly because his size (he was a defensive lineman) made him stand out, and this day was to be no exception. Shortly after we started eating, an upperclassman started to harangue Tim. (I can't quote what he said, because this is a family publication.) What attracted the Cadre's attention was that Tim was taking normal sized bites (at least normal for Tim) out of his hot dog. Apparently, rats were supposed to only take small "rat bites" from their food. I'm sure someone merely forgot to tell us this fact. At least, they didn't tell me and Tim.

Anyway, Tim had by this time managed to attract the attention of some more upperclassmen who were "gently" instructing him on the finer points of rat dining etiquette. While this was going on, a mischievous bug caught hold of me, and I started stuffing as much of my hot dog into my mouth as I could. Tim saw this, since he was looking straight at me, and he started laughing. He didn't start laughing out loud, but he was having considerable difficulty keeping a straight face. Of course, this only served to enrage the Cadre further, and they demanded to know what the heck (once again family publication) was so darn (ditto) funny. Fortunately for me, it kept their attention focused on Tim. It was also lucky for me that Tim didn't tell them what he thought was so funny. Great BR, that Tim White!

When we got back to the locker room, Tim said he couldn't believe I had done that. He also called me a few choice names. In the end though, we laughed over the ridiculousness of the whole thing. We also laughed about the thought of how freaked out the Cadre would have been if they had looked across the table and seen me stuffing my face full of hot dog.

47

Regarding Nicknames

W.D. Meola, '52

My class, the class of 1952, is probably one of the most cohesive classes that ever went to the Institute. I do not state this to demean any other class, and in all likelihood would get an argument from any of the classes that have had the fortune to attend this hallowed school. In some fashion that strengthens my point. I wouldn't want any class to think differently of their Brother Rats. Last April of 2002, my Brother Rats and I came to our fiftieth reunion, and the largest number of our Brother Rats of any previous 50th reunion class attended it. Why? There are probably several reasons: 1) we matriculated in 1948 when the draft and the war limited earlier classes; 2) the military was revered instead of reviled and young men were unashamed of it; 3) an excellent education was available at reasonable cost, and payback was simply Commonwealth service in some profession such as the Virginia DOT; and 4) as much as we rejected and railed against them, the third class did a good job molding us into a class. Does anyone remember Johnny Jordan who led that class? You didn't want to get caught by J.J. It's hard to believe he became a Man of the Cloth, but he did and is well thought of by his parishioners.

What it was I'm not sure, except in the fall of 1948, soon after this group of diverse individuals matriculated, some bond had already been inculcated. We were not afraid to call each other by derogatory names or insult each other, because underneath we knew we were accepted and appreciated. Nicknames had a place in binding this class, and the nastier the name the better. If you want conventional nicknames, look in the back of a Funk & Wagnall's dictionary; real zingers aren't complementary. Some I recall: Scurvy Patton, Poot Head Robertson, and Crud Gladstone for example. There were others not so coarse: Goose Janney, Nutz Navas, and Moogoo Magee come to mind. Some nicknames were made because of behavior—Sleepy Carter, for instance; some for what the Keydet could or could not do, for example swim—Fish Harrington. Some pointed out physical characteristics like Red Austermann and Gerdetz for their fiery red hair; Moon (Moonface) Haley, and Foots Hutter for guess what. Others were a contraction or corruption of their name, like Booky Bookman, Porky Portasik, and Mac McCarthy; others originated somewhere else, like at home. We had at least seven Bill's and Bob's, eight Charlie's, seven Jim's, and more than one Chuck, Johnny, Dick, Jack, and Joe. Nicknames served a purpose; they created familiarity and broke down formality, thus tended to bind. Unfortunately, they also could breed contempt. Even though some in my class had fairly crude nicknames, by and large they were flattered by being singled out, and the name stuck. There are two or three nicknames used frequently by Brother Rats that regrettably are not printable.

Standing in ranks as rats, you were often inspected by your corporal who did not hesitate to reprimand when he saw something that was, in his opinion, not good enough. Shoes that needed more elbow grease on the toes, unpressed straight pants, or peach fuzz on the cheek. Some were more lenient and occasionally would overlook something minor. It may be a scuff on the top of your best spit-shined shoes, a spot on your trousers, or a warning to get a haircut. If you were smart his verbal warning was sufficient enough for you to "straighten yourself out." Other corporals just loved to assign you extra duty, like reporting to his room with a new spit-shine on your shoes or memorizing the Rat Bible starting with the copyright through page 10. During my time in the corps, if an upper classman, like your corporal, let you get away with such stuff you were said to have "Smack" with him. Smack could apply to any upper classman who was acting in his duty capacity if he gave you leniency. The other side of that coin is being devoid of "Smack." This is a condition that no Rat wants to be in, but once in, there is no way out until let out of the Rat Line.

Joe McCarthy and I are in the first platoon of "A" company and are standing in ranks at Dinner Roll Call (DRC). Our squad corporal is doing his usual inspection, starting with the first Rat and now is standing in front of Joe McCarthy. Joe's shoes need more attention, and he is feeling the heat from our corporal. The corporal speaks, "Mistoe McCarthy, where have you been with those cruddy shoes?" There is a pause while Joe tries to find an excuse. "Well, speak up Rat." Joe is stammering something. "Louder Mistoe, I can't hear you." There are two Keydets between "Mistoe McCarthy" and me, and I can hear Joe perfectly. Why can't our corporal? It's just part of the "game." I don't remember what excuse Joe had, but the corporal tells Joe to "drive" around to his room before Taps with a shined pair of shoes. Oh! Oh! Now the corporal is in front of me. I am thinking, 'quit picking on Joe.' Stand at attention Rat, he says. I know what attention is but evidently my shoulders aren't back far enough. I shouldn't tell him he is full-of-it, but I can't help it. This considerably disturbs the corporal; he doesn't like Rats to begin with and especially smart-assed ones. I'm told to drive around to his room before Taps also. Joe and I are "going to the same party."

Joe's shoes are approved, and he is told, "Mister Joe, that's the way I want to see them from now on." I am told that I need to start memorizing the Rat Bible and to recite it page by page to him every evening just before Supper Roll Call (SRC) in his room. We are dismissed.

It doesn't matter how well "Dyked out" you are, without "Smack" you are going to have a rough time of it. Joe and I both catch Hell, but I think Joe gets the worst of it. After a few weeks we started calling Joe "Smack." This was a natural and almost too easy, Mac became "Smack" because he had none. The nickname stuck and to this day Joe McCarthy is known as "Smackarthy." About that time, my nickname was "WD"; I guess that was because it's too hard to make anything much out of Meola. Presently Joe reasoned that turn-about was fair play and when I called him "Smackarthy" he called me as "Smeeola." He became "Smack" and I became "Smee." That also stuck. I am known duly as "WD" or "Smee" and I answer to either. I recently called Joe and without realizing it greeted him with, "How're doing Smack?" and this is after fifty some years. No offense is intended, and none taken, and Joe remains one of my closest friends. This is some of the glue that ties this class together. I don't think any of us would change it even if we could.

48

Rice vs. LSU, October 7, 1950

W.D. Meola, '52

Gambling in barracks was not allowed, but in spite of the penalties that were involved to discourage wagering there were those of us who considered the diversion worth the risk both in pleasure, and sometimes financially. Football parlay cards were distributed liberally throughout the barracks. For the uninitiated, a football parlay card (a football card) lists 15 to 20 football games being played the coming weekend, and indicates the *number of points* by which one team is supposed to beat the other. It is called the "point spread," and the object is to circle the team that will win. Choose the team with the points or the other team. By choosing the other team means their score has to be greater than their opponents score *plus the point spread.* Of course the only games listed by the card "operator" are generally the hardest to pick, because the point spread tends to make the games even.

My roommate, J.B. Hyatt, was as enamored by the prospect of winning a few bucks as I was, and, therefore, we were willing to risk a couple of dollars on a football card each Saturday. As second classmen we were earning 90¢ per day for taking ROTC. Each month we received a check for about $27.00 from "Uncle Sam." These were our investment funds.

We had developed a system to determine which teams offered the best odds. We'd add all the points scored *for* Team A, and to those points add the points given up by the other team. Dividing that total by the games played gave us a number. By doing the same thing for Team B, matching the results with Team A, and factoring in the point spread gave us the team we thought was most likely to prevail.

JB and I used to go over to the engineering building "to study," but actually went over to calculate which teams we thought would win. The following will date us: we used the old time calculators with vertical rows upon rows of buttons numbered from one to ten. Some of the calculators had to be cranked by hand;

others had a motor that turned the crank. It didn't matter both worked the same way. Division was done by multiple subtraction, and multiplication by repetitive addition. The dials would spin with each subtraction or addition, and the carriage would lift, and move as the answer was ground out. After extracting the needed information, we'd take it back to barracks, "worked out" our parlay cards, and turned them in.

I usually played a ten-teamer, i.e., attempting to pick the winners of ten different games. JB and I also played a three-teamer card of our best picks. The real odds of picking the winners of ten different games are 1024 to 1, but the parlay odds only paid 150 to 1. No matter, we thought that was pretty good. The fewer teams you picked the lower the odds became. For a three-teamer the odds were about 5 to 1.

On Saturday, JB and I went to Lexington to the pool hall and shot pool, listening to the football scores as they came in. On October 7, as we left the pool hall, and headed for the barracks, I already had seven or eight correct picks. Our three-teamers, our best picks, however, were "dead." In barracks more scores came in. I now have 9 out of 10 correct. I, at least, will get $20. The Rice game was being played in Texas, and at night, so the score would be late. As I recall, Rice was given 7 points on the parlay card, and I had picked Rice. Now it was "lights out" in barracks, and still no word on the Rice game. Either roommates Chuck Haley or Charlie Piper had an idea. He said, "Call the police station, maybe they had heard the score."

"Come on," I retorted, "Yeah, just pick up the phone, call the police, and tell them, 'Hey, I got a parlay card here, and I need a score'."

But, then I thought I don't have to tell them that; just make up a story. It was worth a try. In 1950, the telephones were in the basement. The stair to the basement was just inside Jackson Arch but quite close to the guardroom. Care was required, because using the telephone without permission after Taps was a minor offense worth 3-5 demerits. Who would have thought the police station was a place where one could find out football scores?

When the desk sergeant answered the phone I could hear a radio playing in the background. I told him I had a large bet with a buddy of mine, and then I asked,

"Do you happen to know the score of the Rice-LSU game?"

He hesitated a moment, looking for the score, then came back, and said,

"Rice 35, LSU 20."

"Wow! Really?"

I kind of gasped. I had just won $150.00. In the Mess Hall the next night at SRC, this first classman came up, and slipped me two bills. One was a hundred, the other a fifty. I had never ever held two such bills before. Man, I was rich. My class ring had been placed on order, but I had not yet figured out how I was going to pay for it. The $150.00 solved that problem, and $65.00 bought it. Over the ensuing years, I have played parlay cards from time to time when I have been able to find them but have never ever come close to picking a ten-team winner since.

49

Room Change

Warren Koontz, '53

The class of 1953 returned to Lexington for its 50th reunion in April 2003. It was the first time that my three roommates and I had been together since our graduation day. We had pictures taken in our room on the first stoop during graduation week in June 1953. Therefore, we thought it would be nice to have our picture taken again in our old room. After the old yell for our class in the courtyard of barracks, we went over to our room to have our picture taken. A change had occurred to our room, since it was now a women's bathroom. As Doc Carroll always said," It's not like the old corps, but it never was."

50

Snakes in Barracks

W.D. Meola, '52

This is a story that is not from personal experience, but I can almost certify that the facts are true, and this did happen. Brother Rat John Root Hopkins as long as I have known him has always had sort of an *off-the-wall* personality. This trait served him well during his army career in Korea where he was awarded a Silver Star. I'm not positive, but I believe it was for calling in artillery on his own position being over run by the Chinese. This was after he had sent his men to the rear. I have contacted the VMI Museum, but all I could find out about Root was that he won the Silver Star. They could not tell me the circumstances, and Brother Root probably wouldn't either.

As the story goes, and I have no reason to disbelieve it, BR Root was out in the woods one afternoon and captured two, three or four foot long Indigo snakes. These snakes are not poisonous. Indigo is a very deep dark blue color, but in my opinion they are colored a deep, dark reddish color. It was in the fall, and these poor snakes were looking for a place to hibernate for the coming winter when Root captured them. So, "OK Root, where are you going to keep these snakes?" Root had it all figured out that the snakes could be kept in the humidifier water pan that hangs from the steam radiator on the backside. Hell, it was three years before I even saw a pan behind my radiator, and really didn't know what it was for.

"Hey, Root, how're the snakes making out today?" "They're okay. I think they are going to sleep, and I don't think I'll have to feed them, maybe until spring." "Damn Root, how you going to keep the Institute from finding out about them snakes; man, you can't hang on to them all winter." As it turned out, Root didn't hang on to those snakes all winter, and that's the story.

Every month, the floors on every stoop were mopped and polished by the maintenance people hired by the Institute for just that purpose. The regimen was some day when you are out of your room, they come along with mop and bucket, and your floor is mopped. Soon after mopping, the floor is polished with one of those electric driven floor polishers. This equipment has a circular brush or buffer that contacts the floor driven by an electric motor that sits on top and spins the buffer. The whole thing is controlled by a T-handle. On the handle is a switch to turn the unit on or off. If per chance the unit is switched on when plugged into the wall outlet, all Hell breaks loose, because the polisher doesn't know the buffer is supposed to spin, and generally the opposite occurs, the handle spins around the buffer.

The afternoon that Root's room was mopped, the maintenance man came in and, with his mop, was working it up and down the length on the floor when inadvertently he happened to strike the legs of the radiator a couple of times with his mop. This of course disturbed the snakes. but they settled back down in their humidifier pan to go back to sleep. Close on the heels of the mopper came the floor polisher. Now, the floor polisher had to get under the radiator as best he could, and consequently hit or knocked the legs of the radiator. This disturbed the snakes a second time, and the snakes decided they'd better see what was going on. They now raised their heads above the top of the radiator. The maintenance man was unaware that he had disturbed anything, much less two snakes. To operate the polishing machine, you push down on the handle to make the machine go in one direction and lift up on the handle to make it go in the other direction. The maintenance man continued lifting, and the machine went away from the radiator, pushing down, and it came back, and hit the radiator. All the while the maintenance man was watching the floor, and observing how well the floor was being polished. About this time he observed out of the corner of his eye some movement behind the radiator. The two snakes, now thoroughly agitated, had reared their heads well above the radiator when the polisher operator finally focused on them. He definitely was not fond of snakes and with that let go of the handle of the polisher. The polisher, still energized, continued to run, but now the handle was spinning around the buffer. The spinning, twisting handle whacked and nicked the tables, threw the chairs around, smashed and dented the room lockers and generally made havoc of the room. Finally, when the power cable had been wound around the handle tightly enough it pulled the plug from the wall. The damage was sufficient to keep Root and his two roommates busy cleaning-up for quite some spell afterwards.

Root and his roommates never had their room mopped or polished again for the rest of the year, and the snakes went back to the woods.

51

Snippets

Ray Lawson, '81

Playing Dixie by remote control: Several of us rigged up an elaborate electronic method to play Dixie (a taboo song due to its perceived racist nature) during a moment of silence at New Market Day in 1981. Pretty interesting how we designed, built, and tested the system. It worked, but there was more to the story than met the "ear." Built a transmitter circuit inside of a Shako hat that we could trip by biting the chinstrap to trigger a tape recording of Dixie on top of barracks.

◆ ◆ ◆

A rather interesting story of how we escaped from a tactical officer in the wee hours of the morning upon return from a girl's school.

◆ ◆ ◆

Shooting a laser from the physics building and attracting the attention of the Lexington police. The laser hit a snow bank alongside the road and made it glow red. A nearby police car turned its spotlight on and tried to find us in the physics building.

◆ ◆ ◆

We convinced one cadet that plastic model airplanes were built to scale and were aerodynamically correct. To prove our point, we got him to let us rig it with a model rocket engine and try to fly it off the roof of the engineering building. We launched it, and it went in the general vicinity of the football stadium but it wasn't a graceful flight. We never found its remains.

♦ ♦ ♦

We used the window well at the engineering building to serve as a model rocket missile silo. We slid a two by six between opposite windows, about two floors down, slid rockets out onto the two by six, and launched the rockets. Some hit the building on the way out. Most were fired when a cadet and his girlfriend were standing outside the building. We shot one and the exhaust smoke went in a window below and nearly suffocated a cadet that was studying in one of the lab rooms.

♦ ♦ ♦

I heard this from another cadet while at VMI. One of the civil engineering professors had the unusual habit of coming into class, picking up a piece of chalk, opening a window, and tossing the chalk out. One day he did this, smiled, turned to the class and said, "Class dismissed. I finally got a piece of chalk to land in that water fountain." Don't know if that's true or not.

♦ ♦ ♦

This is a post VMI story that involved one of us from the Dixie stunt. I went to Boston on business and caught up with one of my fellow Dixie stunt people who was in grad school there. He was proud to show off his new car, which was rather beat up and held together by duct tape, but he bought it himself and was pretty proud of it. I found out a couple of months later that his car had been stolen. His girlfriend was driving him to work (in Boston remember) and, going down some obscure side street, they saw his car in someone's driveway. He had his keys with him and stole his car back. What are the odds of that happening?

52

Spirit Ball

Eddie Fall, '59

In the Fall of '58, the VMI Corps was looking for another great football season. '57 was undefeated. We met VPI in Roanoke on Thanksgiving Day. The team could have gone to a bowl game but turned it down. In '58, the Corps felt we had a great chance to repeat it.

The first two games were winners. The third game against Villanova, Bobby Ross broke his ankle, which had a far greater effect than anyone realized. The spirit in barracks went down like a sinking ship.

Donnie Dreelin, Baldy Fall, Curt Klockner, and Jud Struck formed the spirit committee. We were First Classmen, and we wanted to raise the spirit of the Corps, hoping this would build up the football team. We did things like dressing Donnie Dreelin as a Cavalier, and he rode a mule into the station in Norfolk, Virginia, before the game with the University of Virginia. We won.

William and Mary tied us, and we felt we really had to stick with the team. We had a big game with Citadel and our winning streak was at 18. The spirit committee went to Col. Glover Johns and told him our wish to rent a Pete's taxi and drive down to Citadel with the canon we shot off when VMI scored. Col. Johns gave us a man-to-man talk, telling us he knew we would drink while traveling and asked that one man stay sober to drive. We gave our word that we would follow the rules.

We left Lexington at 4:30 p.m. Friday. The game was Saturday evening, so we had time. Our first stop was Charlotte, North Carolina, at Queens College, a girl's school. One of us knew a girl there, so we all got dates and went to a local park. We were sitting on picnic tables, drinking beer, and trying to make love to our dates when Donnie Dreelin decided there was too much light from the park's electric lights. Up the tree goes Mr. Donald Dreelin, and on his stomach he crawls out on a limb. He was trying to swing a stick at the light to break it. Suddenly, the limb breaks and down comes Brother Rat Dreelin. As he hit the ground with the limb on top of him, the police came out of the bushes yelling at us to put our hands up. Dreelin was out cold and no one seemed to know it. We finally convinced the police he was hurt. They called an ambulance, and Dreelin went to the hospital. Eddie Fall, Curt Klockner, and Jud Struck got sent to the police station. The FPI had seen the taxi, and while looking in the windows, saw the 105 howitzer simulator on the back seat. They thought we were there to blow up schools—remember that integration was a big subject in the late '50's and early '60's. After the three of us told the same story and a call was made to Col. Johns at VMI. At 2:00 a.m. they released us and made us pour two quarts of whiskey down the drain.

The three of us went to the hospital to try to find Dreelin. We found his room, and by the grace of God, no bones were broken (he fell about 20'), but his insides were really shaken up. The doctors said he would have to stay in the hospital about a week. We got a room, slept for eight hours, and headed on our way to the Citadel. We only fired the cannon once—we got beat 14-6. Citadel scored twice on fumbles by VMI. Our winning streak was over, and we had VPI in about ten days (we played on Thanksgiving.)

In all, this was a lost weekend. My roommate Donnie Dreelin was in a hospital some 200 miles away, and Bob Ross was upset about being hurt and his team losing and breaking the winning streak. Fortunately, life at VMI does not allow you to worry about what is in the past. We had too much to do each day in the future. By the way, the spirit committee did not do any good on Thanksgiving Day: We had a two game losing streak now, but one thing happened in the VMI-VPI game that I will never forget:

VMI was down seven points and Bill Nebraska was not having a good day throwing. Coach McKenna asked Bob Ross if he could play. Of course his answer was "yes." Bob hobbled out on the field, and the entire Corps of Cadets stood up and cheered for five minutes. Tears came to my eyes—I had a great deal of respect for Bob Ross, and the one thing the Institute had been teaching for four years came to be true: "The Spirit." By the scoreboard, we lost, but we also won something that Thanksgiving.

53

State Police to the Rescue

Bill Old, no class year provided

Sometime midway through my rat year, I traveled with the swimming team to UVA. At that time, we traveled in a pair of station wagons. The team arrived safely, and I'm sure we won the meet. Afterwards, we had some free time.

When I arrived at the appointed rendezvous, there were no teammates and no station wagons. I waited around for a while until it became apparent that I was the only VMI swimmer in Charlottesville. I called barracks, incognito, and inquired as to whether the team had returned. I was informed that they had.

My dilemma was to get back to the Institute without getting any of the upperclassmen in trouble for leaving me. To a young Rat, that was a big concern. I also needed to make it back before the 11 p.m. stick check.

I called the state police to see if they had anyone headed west. I was told to meet a trooper at the local Texaco station in five minutes. The trooper met me, and we headed for Lexington faster than I had ever traveled on a highway. The trooper called ahead and another car met us at Fairfield.

I had just over sixteen miles to travel in just over ten minutes in order to be on time (also a big deal to a young Rat.)

At 11 p.m., I was studying Shakespeare in one of the classrooms.

At practice the next day, I found out that each of the two team drivers thought I was in the other car.

54

Tanks for the Memories

Houston H. (Tex) Carr, '59

On another occasion, after some disagreement, the armor guys from VMI borrowed the tanks and ran over the grassy knoll in front of the colonnade (at W&L); you know, the one they showed on TV when they were doing the Lexington, VA thing. Made real nice ruts. After that, I think they locked the keys of the tanks up at night.

55

Thanksgiving Day, 1951

W.D. Meola, '52

When I was at the Institute, VMI and VPI played a football game at Victory Stadium in Roanoke, Virginia, on Thanksgiving Day every year. It was always in Roanoke. Like Texas always plays Oklahoma in Dallas, or Georgia plays Florida in Jacksonville. Victory Stadium in Roanoke was considered a neutral field. Although I think Roanoke was more a VPI town than it was for the Institute, while I was at the Institute, we never lost to VPI. Now, however, the two schools are in different football worlds.

After BRC or Breakfast Roll Call the Institute allowed us to go to Roanoke at our leisure as long as we got to our assembly area at the Hotel Patrick Henry on South Jefferson Avenue by 11:30 a.m. As it turned out, not every cadet went to the football game. Some stayed in Lexington, probably because they were on the Gim List, i.e., sick call. Regardless, the Institute had arranged for buses to take us to Roanoke. They lined up on Letcher Avenue, and when one was full it left for Roanoke and the game. The reason we had to assemble at the Patrick Henry was so we could march the mile or so to the stadium as the Corps of Cadets. Before going to our seats, we'd march onto the field and give an Old Yell for our team, and some disparaging yell for the VPI cadets sitting on the other side of the stadium.

Naturally, being given the opportunity to go to Roanoke unchaperoned, we considered this an opportunistic time to engage in a bit of tippling. The problem was finding a bar and grill in some obscure location, so we could quaff a beer or two in relative unobserved security. This was no easy task but always successful. I guess we got to Roanoke about 9-9:30 a.m. and were sitting in an out-of-the-way beer joint at about ten a.m. This gave us an hour to have a beer, and a half an hour to get back to meet the rest of the corps for the march to the stadium. We figured the fresh air walk to the Patrick Henry assembly area would dilute the smell of alcohol enough so a Tack Officer couldn't detect it.

As I approached my brother rats, I was in for a surprise. Some of them ran up to me and accused me of getting caught drinking. I said, "What do you mean? No one saw me drinking." "Well, someone must have, cause you're on report," someone replied. I could only tell them that I didn't know how I could have been caught drinking, because I didn't see anyone that would have reported me. Then I added, "How come I was the only one to get reported. I wasn't alone." That satisfied the guys in my company. But when I got to the stadium, a swarm of incredulous and down cast brother rats surrounded me. They all swore I had been reported back at the Institute for drinking. Some saw the report; I definitely had been "boned" for drinking. I could not figure out how I could be boned and not know it. I sat through the game in a deep funk. My brother rats were down on me, because for the first time in *our* history at the Institute, we weren't on pledge. The whole class was really looking forward to a year without going on pledge. Now, in order to "save my butt," they'd have to go back on pledge, or I'd be dismissed. At this point it looked pretty bad for "WD." This would be a Special Report, and, because I actually had been drinking, I could not, with honor, deny it.

A little information about pledging. An account of the beginning of class pledge is described in Col. Couper's book "One Hundred Years at VMI." In bygone days, if one of your brother rats was caught drinking, he would automatically be dismissed. At the Institute's pleasure he *may* be reinstated the next year but would not graduate with his brother rats. Drinking was probably a problem from the beginnings of the Institute, because whiskey could be made at home and became commonplace. One of the earliest classes saved one of their popular brother rats from dismissal by pledging. An agreement was reached with the Institute. The whole class pledged not to drink for the rest of the year if this brother rat was allowed to stay in school. Pledging is only effective when you, *and each of your brother rats*, have signed the pledge. All brother rats sign or it isn't executable, and the brother rat is dismissed. Since it's inception, according to Col. Couper, the pledge has always been signed.

Back to the story: The game was over, and although I was happy we won 20-7, my mind was preoccupied with being boned for drinking. I was pretty certain I had not been seen drinking while in Roanoke. But how and why was I put on report for doing so? I concluded the report was a mistake; however, I could not disavow that I had been drinking, because I had. I decided the first thing I'd do when I returned to the Institute was to go to the guardroom and check the report.

As it turned out, I didn't have to. The report was incorrect. One of my brother rats had stayed in Lexington and was caught drinking by one of the faculty. The faculty member told this BR to report himself for drinking when he got back to barracks. To ensure he was put on report, the faculty member went to the guardroom before my BR did. Confused, the faculty member reported "Meola" instead of my BR for drinking. When my brother rat got to the guardroom, the mistake was corrected; he took my name off report and put himself on. This all happened before I got back to barracks. I don't remember who may have told me that a correction had been made, but now there was no need for me to jeopardize myself by going to the guardroom to query the report. The jeopardy was this: had the OD asked if I had been drinking, I would have had to answer that I had. Of course, that OD would have eternally headed my S-list.

Let me say, it took some personal courage to do what this brother rat did, and I will forever be thankful for his honesty. It could have been "Meola" instead of my brother rat for which the class pledged. Let there be no doubt in anyone's mind, as far as I was concerned, there was little hesitation in me signing pledge for him.

56

The Bomb and the Mullion

W.D. Meola, '52

As near as I can recall, my rat year roommates were David Harvey, Charlie Moore, Pete Meekins, and Mark Hillman, and we roomed in the tower room on the east side of barracks. Along with some 236 other classmates, we were known as Rats, and rats are the lowest forms of life in barracks. As a matter of fact, we weren't even considered a class yet and wouldn't until we ran the gauntlet in May. As anyone who has been to VMI will tell you, Rats lived on the fourth stoop (i.e. floor) third classmen on the third stoop, Seconds on the second' etc. Third classmen are charged with disciplining the Rats, and most all Third classmen take this very seriously. Third classmen have only recently themselves gotten out of the Ratline and now are ready to "dish it out," to show the Second and First classmen that they can handle these new rats. The Ratline? Oh yes! Rats are to walk as if they were rats. They walk along the edge of the stoop until stopped by the corner stairs, then to the wall around the stairs and back out to the edge. Rats are not to loiter on the stairs and must do them in double time, either up or down.

Back to my story. The Third classmen below our room were rather conscientious regarding Rat discipline. If or when we Rats made too much racket, which was transmitted through the concrete floor, these Third classmen would signal us above by ramming a broom handle against the ceiling of their room hard enough to be heard in our room above. Normally, this was some kind of *"whump, thump, wham,"* followed by a chorus of "quiet up there you rats."

After some weeks of this annoyance, we decided a bit of surreptitious retaliation was in order. We had obtained a few of what I called "cannon crackers," a firecracker about the size of your little finger with a fuse that seemed to be made out of thick twine. The plan was to toss it out of the window so it would explode at or near the Third classmen's window. A firecracker is only a firecracker, but when it has been confined in a tin can and friction taped to the size of a small softball the concussion can be phenomenal. In the late 1940's, Scotch tape could be bought in a steel metal can about 4-5 inches in diameter and maybe an inch high. It had a cover that could be twisted off, and the metal was thin enough that a small hole could be put in it just large enough to fit the cannon cracker's fuse. Once the cracker was in the can and the cover replaced, it was then taped with the friction tape until only the fuse showed.

Now everything was ready. The Third classmen were in their room below, and the "bomb" was all taped up. Since we had to throw the bomb out the window, we opened it wide. VMI barracks windows are about thirty inches wide and about six feet high. There are two of them, a left hand and a right hand one. Either one or both can be opened into the room when fresh air is needed. When shut, they are latched to a mullion in the middle of the window opening. With the bomb in my right hand, and C.F. Moore or Don Harvey there to light the fuse, I was set to throw it. (Don't know whether Meekins or Hillman were there.) The three of us were at the other end of the room nearly as far away from the windows as we could be, since we did not want to be seen anywhere by them. The plan was not to be in the room just in case. If we weren't in the room, the Thirds would have to look somewhere else for the culprit.

"Light the fuse Charlie, light it." Charlie lit the fuse, and I waited a short fraction of a second to make sure the explosion would occur at or near our Third classmen's window, and then I threw the bomb. The bomb flew from my hand, and arced toward the window; it was a perfect throw. My aim was perfect, that is for the mullion; it was hit squarely, and the bomb bounced back into the room. Charlie, Don, and I all tried to get out of the room first, before the bomb exploded, but we wouldn't fit together. Neither of us would let the other out first, and the bomb exploded with a horrendous boom. It left a white mark on the floor, filled the room with smoke and litter and made our ears ring for hours. The white mark remained there until the end of the year, although the maintenance men, tried as they would, couldn't eradicate it.

The Third classmen below us? Whump, whump, wham, thump, bam!!! "What the Hell you doing up there, Rats? Quiet down! Any more noise, and all you are going up before General Committee." Needless to say, the rest of the time we roomed there, we were especially careful not to rile any Third classmen, especially those below us.

◆ ◆ ◆

After writing this story it occurred to me that I was *not* the one who threw the bomb, but I don't remember who did. It really doesn't matter who threw the bomb; it never got out the window. Another problem we had was cleaning up the room. There must have been a thousand pieces, and some may still be lying around to this day.

57

The Cadre Sergeant

David Schwab, '73

My cadre sergeant was my example of how to be a good cadre sergeant. I was the first ranking sergeant in Alfa Company in 1971 and with it came a big responsibility: training Rats.

Since I was the ranking sergeant in the first line company, I got the first squad of Rats during matriculation. They were all football players—something I hadn't counted on.

Not only were they in better shape than most of their Brother Rats, they had been at VMI for a week or so, knew some of the routine and had all the upperclassmen on the football team looking out for them. I hadn't counted on that, either.

I had prepared little signs for my Rats, just like my cadre sergeant had done for me in 1969. Apparently the First Classmen on the football team didn't find it amusing; they persuaded me to remove them. They mentioned something about "trifling with a Rat" being a First Class privilege.

58

The Definitive Cannonball Burial Story

Leroy Hammond, '57

Here are a few more details to fill out the story from Volume I (of *Memories of VMI*) of how the cannonball ended up partially buried in the Old Courtyard: the cannonball was kidnapped by Brother Rats of mine from the illustrious Class of 1957 ("The Last of the Old Corps—Beat Catawba, Hey!!"), during our First Class Year, after making involved engineering calculations as to its weight and doing some breaking/tearing strength testing in the CE Department labs on blankets to see how many thicknesses would be needed to be able to haul it. The *original* intent was to make an editorial statement about the disdain felt by the Corps about a particularly "chicken" Officer-in-Charge. This worthy had just purchased a new red sports car, and the band of guerillas had gone so far as to position the car in Marshall Arch and had brought the cannonball to the 4th stoop directly above the Arch, with a view toward seeing if dropping it into the car would send the cannonball *all the way* through the car to the bricks, or just make a lovely and most satisfying dent.

Discretion proved the better part of valor at the dead-last minute, and the cannonball was taken around the 4th stoop into Old Barracks and dropped into the Courtyard in the vicinity of room 150…the tale includes the little fillip that a Rat (would have been Class of 1960) was leaving his dyke's room…Room 150…and had reached the stoop-rail just as the cannonball impacted two feet in front of him…he thought World War III had commenced.

The cannonball buried itself better than halfway into the ground. It took about a week to extract it, as the Buildings and Grounds crew had to bring in a back-hoe and dig a trench all the way around the cannonball so they could get under it to remove it…at certain times of the year, if you know exactly where to look…which I do…you can still see the faint shadow of "Ground Zero," as the soil they put back was better than what they took out and the grass there is a shade greener than that surrounding the site.

The truth of the eventual location (some to this day wish we had gone ahead with the sports-car plan) and depth of burial was captured for posterity and there is proof positive in the 1957 Bomb, of which I was honored to be the Editor.

Even our Brother Rats didn't know the whole story until our 35th or 40th Reunion (we're getting old…who can remember numbers!), when the Leader of The Guerilla Band, whose name will be kept under wraps (it was NOT me!!) lest he be boned retroactively, outlined the entire tale…

59

The Hook and the Tree

W.D. Meola, '52

Generally on Wednesdays, Saturdays, and Sundays cadets had some free time. Often it was spent practicing with an athletic team, such as the varsity football team or maybe an intramural team. In the late forties, and early fifties, the Corps of Cadets was made up of six companies divided into two battalions. For each intramural sport, each company fielded a team that played teams from all the other companies. The over-all winners in each sport accrued points toward the Garnett-Andrews Cup. All companies coveted this trophy, because it signified they were the best for the year. When there were no other pastimes to occupy a cadet, and the parade ground (or "parade" as it was known) was open (i.e., no parades or other institute activities were using the parade), it was permissible to practice your golf swing, and hit a golf ball around the perimeter. Now the parade is several hundred yards long, and almost as broad as it was long. The grass was kept mowed, and it was a good place to whack a golf ball without fear of losing it.

It was springtime; the sun was out, and I had a six iron and a golf ball. I could hit a six iron about 150 yards, so with three or four shots, I had reached the other end of the parade ground. In the early fifties, there was a faculty home with a large tree alongside of the house at the corner of the VMI parade ground and Letcher Avenue, close to Limit Gates. The tree was an evergreen variety and had a thick profusion of branches and pine needles with a trunk stretching maybe 70 or 80 feet high. The house was about 150 yards from me so to ensure missing the house I aimed *far to the left* of the tree. Much to my Angst, after I hit the ball, it curved into the top of the tree. It then tumbled its way through the branches until it reached the ground. Under the tree the ball dropped near two of the faculty member's children. As I approached the tree to recover my ball, the faculty member came out of the house and asked for my name. I told him, "Meola, W.D., Sir." He then said, "I am boning you for hitting a golf ball so as to endanger children." There was little doubt that this would be a Special Report. The minimum penalty for a "special" is Ten, Two, and Ten, i.e., 10 demerits, 2 weeks confinement, and 10 penalty tours. To accumulate over 15 demerits per grading period costs you one penalty tour per demerit up to 20 demerits. Over 20, and the rate was two penalty tours per demerit. Having 10 demerits meted out at once usually put you over 15 demerits and additional penalty tours.

As if a special report wasn't bad enough, it had to be answered by endorsement and signature, then in person in front of the Commandant of Cadets, Colonel Oliver B. Bucher. The colonel was a no nonsense soldier who knew the VMI Blue Book of regulations forward and backward, and could quote it "chapter and verse." However, there was no one fairer than Colonel Bucher, and although to stand before him with your explanations was not for the fainthearted, you could be sure to be treated fairly and in accordance with the regulations.

On the special, I wrote essentially what I have described above, except as I related my explanation, I animated it. Using my right arm in a sweeping right hand motion I told the colonel, "......and the ball hooked into the tree." He looked at me as I was giving my explanation then questionably repeated it with the same type of arm motion I had used. He said, "Meola that's not a hook. You sliced the ball into that tree," and as he tore up the special he said, "Now, get out of here." "Yes, Sir", and I got out of there.

I had prided myself on the ability to write explanations for special reports, and on occasion used to do so for my roommates. This time, however, it wasn't what I had written so much as the sweep of my arm that got me off the proverbial "hook."

60

The Inscrutable Dr. Chang

Erwin Hanke, '71

As is often/usually the case when memories such as these are recounted to the principal player some thirty years after the fact in Moody Hall, the protagonist admitted no memory of the event, though he did not deny it either.

First, some background information is necessary for those not aware of Economics, the Early Years. I believe that for many years, Col Morrison '39 *was* the Economics Dept. The first class to be granted the Bachelor of Arts in Economics degree was in 1968, with twenty-one graduates. There were thirty-two in 1969, so I theorize Col Morrison believed the program was too easy. The result was that 1970 saw only thirteen Econ's stroll the stage and only fifteen graduated in 1971. I don't know exactly how the numbers ran after that, but I believe it was some time before Economics and Business became the force on "campus" that it is today. Back in 1971, if the corps had been divided into the two camps of "engineers" and "liberal artists," it would have been conceded by all that Econ majors were *at least* honorary engineers.

Now, Col Morrison had received his Ph.D. from UVA, and I believe his goal was to make sure that anyone who survived his program would be able to go toe to toe with anyone out of UVA, Harvard, or Chicago. I'm not saying that he had an "our mission is attrition" mindset, but that seemed to be the effect. Among those that he recruited to carry out his plan to have VMI recognized as the Wharton of the Southeast was Dr. James Lih Yong Chang.

At this point, I will admit to the facts of my own case. I had been a transfer *into* Econ (a distinction shared by only one of my BR's), but it was not a happy marriage, rather one, I thought, of practicality. I may very well be the only cadet to actually be conferred the BA in Economics without having ever received a course grade above a "C" within the major. Here is my story.

By the last semester of my First Class year, I had only one Economics class left to take, a seminar in International Economics, with Dr. Chang. I was taking only fifteen hours so this was it, my last, best chance to shine in my major.

I had what was a good start, for me. A "B" average at midterm and a "B" going into the final. I studied hard to master the abstractions of economics that had been my bane over the years. I had taken all of my finals and had gotten all of my other grades; I had made the Dean's List for certain. (Naturally, this event didn't have quite the thrill it would have had in previous semesters, as there would be no extra weekends to enjoy off post *after* graduation.) I went to the bulletin board where grades were posted, for all to see. (No longer the case, I understand. Not protective of the fragile psyches of the "students.") Found the course listing, scanned down to my name, over to view the grades. A "B" on the final! At last, the grail would be mine! Scanned over to the right to savor the satisfaction of the final grade....

A "C!" Huh! What? Even with this "C," I had earned that hollow victory of the Dean's List, but I didn't understand this turn of events. I had to see Dr. Chang.

I found him outside of his office in the "root cellar" (as we affectionately referred to the offices of the Econ Dept., nestled within the very bowels of Scott Shipp Hall). Though in a hurry to return home to Charlottesville, he acquiesced to helping his now former-student through this simple alphabetic-mathematical calculation. I related my incomprehension as to how my final grade in my final economics class had been derived.

"Dr. Chang, I had a B going into the final, right?"

"Yes, Mr. Hanke," he replied.

"I got a B on the final, yet I received a C for the course. Why didn't I get a B?" I asked.

"But, Mr. Hanke, you are a C student."

61

Under Arrest

W.D. Meola, '52

The date was June 9, 1952, and the next day I was to receive my diploma as a civil engineer and graduate from the VMI. I was not a terrific student. I might have been classified as an average student as I ranked about 70th out of some 150 graduates in our class. But as some 240 had matriculated with our class, I figured I hadn't done too badly. But I remember this date not because I was going to graduate, but because I spent the night under arrest. Here is the story.

As first classmen, we were allowed to have a car for the last week or two of school, and I had a car. I had a date for Finals with a girl named Charlotte Crickenberger, and after the Hop, we drove to a spot where we could talk and do what young couples normally do when they are alone, and undisturbed. Thanks to strenuous encouragement from Charlotte, I was a total gentleman. After the dance was over, cadets (at least First classmen) were allowed to be out until 2 a.m. After having parked with Charlotte for some time, I drove back to the barracks shortly before 2 a.m. and parked the car near the end of New Barracks. As I recall, it was warm. I sat on the curb with the passenger's door open, and Charlotte sat in the car while we enjoyed each other's company until I had to report to my room. We were telling things to each other about our two lives that were both funny and enlightening. At times, one or both of us would laugh out loud. As it turned out, not a very smart thing at 2 a.m. in the morning.

The place where we parked was close to the Dean of Faculty, General Anderson's residence; too close. Time was passing, and little did we notice the hour, which happened to be very near the time that I had to be in my room. I heard a voice behind me coming from the second floor of the general's home. The Dean had come to his bedroom window and wanted to know, "Who's that down there?" As has befallen me several times during my tenure at VMI, I responded with the ritual, "Meola, WD, Sir," but this time I added, "and date." I thought this might soften his obvious ire. He told me we were making a disturbance, and I was to go the guardroom and report myself under arrest. I said "Sir? Under arrest?" The Dean indicated I was to be under arrest for making too much noise at 2 a.m. I don't quite know how I felt,…scared mostly. Would I now be able to graduate? Would I be dismissed? Maybe the Dean would give me some penalty tours, but there was no time left in the school year to work them off. I did have the rest of the night but I didn't know what the penalty would be. Also, would I lose my stripes? I was the lowest ranking officer, but was still proud to wear stripes. My God, what a predicament! To be placed under arrest the last night of my career at VMI would devastate my mother, and particularly my father. He had always wanted me to go to West Point, but all I could get was a third alternate, and I was not accepted. If I failed to graduate from VMI, it would have sorely hurt him.

I had to say good night to Charlotte, and I truly don't know how the girl got to her room at the tourist home where she was staying. I must have either driven her there or let her take the car. Time has diminished that memory. I reported myself to the guardroom and went to my room. I told my roommates that I had been placed under arrest for disturbing General Anderson's peace, and I had no idea what was to become of me. They indicated I'd probably be released for graduation in the morning, but they also said the Institute might just send me my diploma if I couldn't make the graduation ceremony. I didn't sleep well at all the rest of the night.

The next morning my Dad called to find out about the times for the family to be where they were supposed to be and when. I told Dad I was under arrest but that I didn't do anything I thought was beyond the regulations, and that I might have to walk some penalty tours before I could get my diploma and leave. I told him not to worry and lied to him that this was just temporary. Shortly after talking to him, however, I was summoned to the guardroom by the PA system on top of the Sentry Box. I gulped, said goodbye to my roommates, and headed for the guardroom to face up to my fate. After reporting, the OD told me that General Anderson had called the guardroom, and I was being released from arrest with no penalty.

I felt like a prisoner sentenced to hang who just had gotten a reprieve. I don't think there was any chance of actually floating off the stoop but I felt light as a feather. As soon as I could, I called my Dad who by this time was sitting on pins and needles and told him I would graduate with my class, and things were as they should be. Needless to say, this escapade has become close to the top of the Meola family history. To the end of Dad's days, he could not forget it, and neither have I.

62

VMI Commander Trips

Houston H. (Tex) Carr, '59

I had the good fortune to become a member of the VMI dance band, *The Commander*, early in my Rat year. I played baritone saxophone plus hauled and toted stuff, like a good rat. We had a great band, five saxophones, two trombones, two trumpets, a real non-electric bass fiddle, piano, and singer. Later we added a guitar. This was the era of the big band sound, and we did quite well. *Blue Star* was our theme song, and we could make the girls swoon with our sound.

While we played at Sem and W&L, my favorite trips were to Foxcroft, Hollins, and Sullins College (Bristol, VA). Sullins, like Sem, was high school and junior college, and peopled by girls from well-to-do families. The trip down there took several hours, and along the way we managed to change into civvies. Some of the guys even managed to get hold of some (heaven forbid) beer. During our First Class year, Mike Maupin (sax and clarinet) figured he was in charge; Rob Summers (sax and clarinet) was business manager and seemed to always drive the bus; Russ Crew (trombone) was keeper of refreshments, and Jack Christie (piano) was the onboard music leader. The trip to the dance job was fun as we were leaving Barracks, got out of uniform, and even dined in a regular restaurant. The trip back was very different, as we tried to sleep on an old yellow school bus after we had played for four hours. Some had help sleeping from Sandman Budweiser.

At one restaurant, we were sitting around killing time until the dance job began, and the waitress started to talk with us. I think several of us were wearing our class sweaters, and she asked about it and our rings. Someone said they were magic rings and that the wearer could make it do tricks. Not believing the storyteller, she said he would have to prove his claim. With that, he took the ring off, spun it on the stone top, and at the right moment, snapped his fingers and the ring flipped, obediently up on its other end. Considering the shape and weight distribution of the ring and that the '59 ring was the largest and heaviest in VMI history, any '59 ring would do this trick, all you had to know was how long it took to flip. On an earlier trip, one of the guys showed off his silver rat ring as our class ring, again, to impress our waitress. Don't think this ever did any good, but we were impressive.

63

VMI Prelude to Real Life

Erwin Hanke, '71

One of the many blessings experienced by students of VMI, not shared by matriculants of other schools, is participating in the learning experience that is derived from protecting the property of the Commonwealth of Virginia, i.e. Guard Duty.

It was in the dark days of February in 1969 that I, a luckless and excuseless Third, thought myself to be without recourse to answering the call of the Mother "I" to "protect and serve" as a simple private on the stellar Echo Company Guard Team of 3-4 Feb. I had harbored hopes of wangling "supernumerary," that sweet spot on the guard team that requires two privates to participate in Guard Mount, but precious little else unless there was a full-scale attack by Hokies, Minks, or Chi-coms (the latter the most likely of the three.) Alas, I did not enjoy the favor of First Sergeant Santoro or whoever was responsible for perpetrating that travesty; two Seconds pulled rank on me. Is there anything sadder than performing sentinel duty in the middle of winter, pounding the cold, hard bricks in the dead of the night, not as a rat (when you are inured to that sort of abuse), but as a Third? Well, of course there is, and, sadly enough, I have those stories to tell just as you do, but it was still a pitiful state of affairs. In fact, this story gets worse.

Now, as it happened, my call to guard duty came just days before my required Army physical, a prerequisite to formal enrollment in ROTC, that all-important step that ensured that 1) you were not subject to being drafted out of school and 2) you would receive a stipend for your commitment to being a full-fledged participant in Senior ROTC come the fall as a small cog in the American War Machine. A requirement of the physical was that I could not wear contact lenses for a period of three days prior to the vision test on February 7. I was fine for Guard Mount and through the rest of the day, but could not wear the contacts from the next day on. As my vision was in the 20/500+ range, wandering around barracks without visual correction of some sort would not be inconvenient; it would be downright dangerous, even with an *unloaded* M-1. But no problem, I had a pair of glasses, right?

Not to quibble, but…yes and no. While I was home over Christmas furlough, I had gone to the optometrist for my pre-examination examination. The verdict was that, once again, my prescription needed to be changed. So I left my one pair of regular glasses in the loving hands of my dear, caring, and too-busy-to-get-right-on-this mother, a consideration which I had not given any thought to until arising at 05-early on the last leg of my tour as guard. What I did have was a pair of silvered, wire-rimmed, *very* dark green prescription sunglasses, which I proceeded to put on so that I might get dressed in the dark of the pre-dawn, then carefully felt my way down the stoops and the stairs to the guard room.

I was making pretty good progress until I hit the first stoop sally port, approaching the Commandant's office. Coming toward me from the direction of Jackson Arch was someone about my height, but wearing a green uniform. Instead of simply returning my snappy rifle salute (M-1 armed as I was in overcoat with white belt, cartridge box and bayonet,) he stopped me to ask, "What the #*" I thought I was doing wearing "hippie" sunglasses while on guard duty? I tried to answer his question with the facts of the matter, but it became painfully obvious that his question was rhetoric in nature and the only real information that he required was my name. Talk about a bad way to start your day…I don't think he liked guard duty any more than I, but rather than looking for someone to commiserate with about having to be up so early, he simply wanted to make sure that someone was enjoying it less than he was.

I took off the glasses and felt my way along the wall to the guardroom, where I reported my unhappy plight to the Sergeant of the Guard. While basically unsympathetic but somewhat amused, he gave me some unobtrusive duty for the remainder of our tour. As I pondered the possible results of my early morning interview, I thought, "After all, how bad could it be?"

How about finding a Special Report sitting on your desk the next morning instructing:

Cadet Hanke, E., Class 1971, you will answer by endorsement hereon the following delinquency: Conduct unbecoming a cadet, i.e., wearing hippie sunglasses while on guard, 4 February, 1969.

Stacy C. Harris
Major, VA Militia
Assistant Commandant

Conduct unbecoming! Quick…to the Blue Book…What? The big "D" to Number 1! For having bad eyes, bad timing, and bad luck (not to mention a baadd pair of sunglasses?) Conduct unbecoming. I thought that was for, like, being caught driving drunk in civilian clothes through the mayor's front yard, tearing up his wife's prized Dusty Gold Abyssinian roses with his fifteen-year old daughter, Misty, half-naked in the front seat of a stolen car! How was I going to tell my poor mother that her pride and joy first born son had been kicked out of college, probably about to be drafted and sent to 'Nam to be killed or horribly maimed for life because she had forgotten to get his eyeglass prescription filled?

Due to the nature of the "crime," I had to answer this report to the Commandant, Col France. During the period of my standing at attention outside of the Commandant's office, I believe I sweated off about ten percent of my body weight. When the "opportunity" to answer the report came, I entered the office, placed my cap under my left arm as I approached the colonel's desk and saluted. When asked how I answered the report, I responded with the cadet's cry for mercy, "Correct, but I wish to explain." To *my* credit, I did not tear up, fall to the floor, or beg for mercy; I just gave my story. To *his* credit, Col France did not ask to see the curious glasses or lecture me about my wicked, hippie tendencies, nor did he order me to change into my coatee for a stroll across the parade ground to Smith Hall for a private audience with His High Holiness, Gen Shell. What he did do was rewrite the delinquency to: "Failure to comply with provisions of par. 215 VMI regulations, ref. Sick Call." The penalty assessed was 5–1–0, five demerits, one week's confinement and no penalty tours. That wasn't so bad, especially when I had been staring down the barrel of a "#1," but what did *get* me was his telling me that I should have had myself placed on the "gim" list due to my inability to perform regular duty during the three days; I would have avoided all of that trouble, *and* I wouldn't have had to serve on the guard team at all! *Now* he tells me. I'm *so sure* that my permit to get "all duty" would have been approved 'cause my Mommy hadn't sent my glasses.

It is said that the common difference between School and Real Life is that in School, they teach you the lesson, and then they give you the test. In Life, you get the test first, and you learn the lesson from that. How about that; VMI was just like Real Life! And the lesson? "Don't wear *hippie* sunglasses while on guard duty." Message received. I haven't done it since.

64

Welcome to the RDC

David Schwab, '73

I still have my first card to the RDC. It reads, "A personal invitation has been extended to the above Rat to attend the Christmas RDC party."

It reads further, "Present this at door. Uniform—fatigues."

The signature at the bottom is "J.M.Hall."

Trip to the Regimental S1.

The Regimental S1 was a man to be feared, so when he extended his personal invitation to visit him at regimental headquarters during RQ, I was terrified.

All I could think of that evening in 1969 was, "What can I do to avoid this?" Poison came to mind, but I rejected the idea as too extreme.

The experience could have been worse. I ended up performing some physical exercise and answering some Rat Bible questions, while the gentleman strained me. I tried to make it look worse than it really was, figuring he would take it easy on me. I guess I was a bad actor, because he didn't.

My salvation came with CCQ.

65

What Mercedes?

Eads, Matt, '93

As a member of the Class of 1993, we were Rats from Fall 1989 to Spring 1990. As Rats often do, we chose to create and implement a self-motivated "Rat activity" which we hoped would impress our Dykes—the Class of 1990. In fact, we hoped to show them that we were coming together as a Class. So, in all of our wisdom, we chose to take the Class on a self-motivated early morning Rat rifle run.

The morning of the run was a classic Shenandoah misty morning. Not only did our run begin under the cover of darkness, but also the fog and mist around the parade ground were very thick. Our run started out from the front of barracks and took us around the parade ground in front of the Sup's house. Well, on that particular day, an active duty General was visiting Post and was staying at the Sup's house (General Knapp's house at the time.) This visiting General was driving a Mercedes, which was parked against the curb in front of the house.

One of our BR's wore glasses that can only described as extremely thick. With the misty, wet air that was present that morning, this BR's glasses fogged up during the run. Because of the fog on his lenses, this BR lost his way from the running formation and managed to run into the General's Mercedes, thrusting his M-14 right through the back window (I think it was the back window) of the car. The window was a total loss.

Our Class decided to raise money to pay for the damage. When the Class presented the collection to the General, he declined to accept it, because he was so impressed that we had been proactive in coming forward about the accident and raising the money needed to make the repairs.

66

Wrestling at SMA

W.D. Meola, '52

After my experience euphemistically playing Rat football, consisting mainly of performing as the next week's opponent for the varsity, you would think, "Ok, you've had this experience, so now let's get on with our education." However, when I looked over at my Brother Rats at their straining tables, it was incentive enough for me to seek out another training table. I discovered we had a Rat wrestling team and it qualified for training table status. Therefore, although I had not ever wrestled formally (only as kid might do in a scuffle), I signed up for Rat wrestling. I figured if there weren't too many of us Rats signing up, I might have a chance to stay on the team. We must have been "hard-up," because I made the team.

I weighed just over 160 pounds and wrestled in the 165-pound weight class. Col. Sterling Heflin was the coach, and he taught us wrestling holds by demonstration. He would pick out someone from our team and proceed to put the new "hold" on the selected unfortunate. Col. Heflin was no spring chicken, but if you grabbed hold of him, you realized there wasn't any fat there, only rock solid, hard muscle. Often he would say, "Meola, come out here a minute." Then he would grab hold of me, and before I knew it, I was on my back or being tossed like a rag doll. A college wrestling match consists of three periods of three minutes each. For the first period both wrestlers are standing up and trying to "take down" the other. The second period, one wrestler gets on all fours, that is, on his hands and knees. He then is "on the bottom." The other wrestler is "on top" and puts one hand on the arm of the guy on the bottom with the other arm around his torso. The third period, if there is one, the wrestlers are reversed. The one who was on all fours now is "on top."

One particular time I found out how solid this Colonel Heflin was. He had placed himself "on the bottom" and told me to position myself on top. So, with one hand on his left arm and my right arm around his torso, he went on to explain how to break my hold on him. One should quickly throw one's feet forward, roll, and try to stand up. The Colonel said, "On three I'm going to try to break your hold," and then told me to tighten my grip. I thought I already had a tight grip on this old guy, but before I knew it, he was free and on top of me. When successful, as I recall, the guy on the bottom earns one point for breaking the hold. If at the same time he gets on top of the other guy, he earns another two points. In a wrestling match, two points is big and three points almost unbeatable. The Colonel would have earned all three points. Our practices went like that—Colonel Heflin demonstrating and then, for about another half-hour or 45 minutes, we would practice what we had just learned on our teammates.

Practicing, it was better to find someone who was heavier than you. You had to work harder to move him. The other guy learned he had to move quicker, because the lighter guy normally was faster.

A high school came to the Institute for a match. I believe it was Greenwood Academy. Their 165-pound guy was long and rangy, and he was hard to keep in a hold, because he'd stretch those legs and all of a sudden he'd be free. I stayed with him through the first period and the second period but was getting tired. I thought being ahead by a point gave me enough "wind" to beat this guy. But now we're in the third period, and I had to start on bottom. Try as I might, that guy wouldn't let me go. He was collecting a lot of "riding time." Riding time is length of time one wrestler stays on top of the other wrestler. At the end of the match, the one with the most riding time gets points. This can sway the match. As much as I wanted to escape, I couldn't. Finally, I was so tired, I was almost happy he pinned me. I had learned that one needs to conserve energy.

The next match was at Staunton Military Academy (SMA), an away trip all of 30 miles up the road. It was set up so the mat was between the two teams with benches on each side so we faced each other across the mat. Staunton's team captain stood behind his wrestlers, and as each one got up for a match, he would give them a pep talk, a little massaging, a pat on the fanny, and send them out. Across the mat, my opponent was so small, I figured he couldn't weigh more than 145 or 155 pounds. I knew this guy was mine. The 135-pound match was over; we lost it, and SMA's 145-pound guy got up. The captain came over, gave his pep talk, etc., and sent his 145-pound guy out.

After it was over, their coach told our coach that their 155-pound guy was injured and just sitting on the bench. Sort of like an injured football player who dresses without pads. Staunton forfeited that match. So now it was my turn to wrestle. We were behind in score, but I knew I could take my guy and started jumping up and down and rotating my arms to get the juices running. Coach

Heflin would like me winning one. So would I; it would be my first one. I was looking at *our* bench, and when I turned around, their captain wasn't behind their bench.

"What's going on," I thought, and "Where's their captain?" He wasn't behind their bench any more, because he was standing on the other end of the mat facing me. I was wrestling their captain. All the while I was thinking their 155-pound man was my guy; now it was their captain who was my man. That match was pretty short. I never even breathed hard before it was over. I stayed away from him for a while, until I tried to take him down and went for his legs. This was a big mistake. The captain had wrestled some before and probably "baited" me to go for the legs. With my head down rushing toward his legs, he slammed me to the mat turned, me over, and I was looking at the lights. The referee whammed the mat, and the match was history.

I never won any of the three or four matches I wrestled in. They didn't call me *Canvasback* for *nothing*. But I was in pretty good physical condition after Colonel Heflin got through with me. I may not have been a good wrestler, but in my mind success wasn't measured by wins and losses but by getting on the training table. I was in good enough condition to make the track team, and they also had a training table.

67

Ring Figure

Strickler, Edmund R., '62

On Saturday after our Ring Figure in 1960, several of us decided it would be a good idea to have a picnic with our dates. The weather was beautiful, and Goshen beckoned. The only problem was that civilian clothes would be more comfortable than blouses and straight pants. We went to one of our date's motel room and changed into civvies. Now it was time to get supplies, and a grocery store was right around the corner. We grabbed a basket and started with hotdogs, chips and lots of other goodies. We were heading for the beer when there was a tap on someone's shoulder and a young looking man (we were all young then) said that he wanted our names before we left the store. One of us thought it was a "mink" and told him to "Go to hell!" We suddenly realized it was Captain Knapp (later to become Major General Knapp and VMI's 12th superintendent). Thank goodness, he forgave us our mistaken identity and said he was only going to bone us for wearing civilian clothes. Then he told us to go on and have a good time that evening!

Many years later I asked him if we had already placed the beer in our basket but hadn't paid for it, would we have been boned for possession of alcohol and, if so, would it have stuck since it really wasn't ours yet. He said, "I don't know but we would have found out!"

I am certainly glad that I didn't have to find out, as 10-2-40 was much easier to explain to my father than suspension or dismissal would have been.

General Knapp and I still laugh about that incident though it wasn't funny at the time.

Lexicon for the Uninitiate

Bone:	To be charged with demerits and penalty tours for not following the rules and regulations.
BRC:	Breakfast Roll Call.
Breaking Out:	The day when the rats (4th Classman) would get out of the Ratline.
BRF:	Brother Rat Fink.
CIVILS:	Civil Engineering students.
CP:	Class Period.
CQ:	Call to Quarters.
DRC:	Dinner Roll Call.
Dyke Out:	To dress oneself for parade and/or to help to dress one's dyke (1st Classman/big brother) for parade.
Evening Cannon:	At the time the flag was lowered in the evening, the cannon would be discharged.
Little Toot:	A bugle sound meaning that a cadet needed to be in ranks before Little Toot ended.
Mixer Permits:	Permits to attend a dance function such as those that were held at the Southern Seminary.
Number One:	15 demerits, 4 months confinement, 60 penalty tours.
OG:	Officer of the Guard.
On Permit:	Either cadets that were on permit for participation in athletic programs or a permit to leave the Post for an authorized purpose.
Permit Rat:	A rat (4th classman) who participated in an athletic program.
PT:	Physical Training.
Sally Port Sinks:	The lavatories/showers located on each stoop (floor) between old and new barracks.

SMI:	Sunday Morning Inspection.
Southern Sem:	The former Southern Seminary Junior College for women located in Buena Vista.
SRC:	Supper Roll Call.
Stick Check:	A cadet needed to be in his room at the time the guard hit his stick on the door. If not, the cadet would be honor bound to report himself as being absent.
TAC:	A tactical officer who would be in charge of barracks for a particular 24-hour period.

About the Author

Aside from *Memories of VMI, Volumes I and II,* Ursula Maria Mandel, Ph.D., has published *The Good American: A Novel Based on True Events,* and a number of essays and stories. For more information on *Memories of VMI* and on her other publications, please go to her website: *www.ursulamandel.com.*

0-595-29559-2